Cultural Pluralism

Cultural Pluralism

Edited by

Edgar G. Epps
University of Chicago

McCutchan Publishing Corporation
2526 Grove Street
Berkeley, California 94704

ISBN 8211-0412-8
Library of Congress Catalog Card Number 73-17617

Series Foreword

The essays in this collection bring into sharp focus the developments which have made the concept of cultural pluralism the vital force it is today in American society. But Professor Edgar G. Epps, the editor, and his associates help us to see that the imperatives of a pluralistic society have yet to be generally accepted. The authors have all been deeply involved in one way or another in the struggles to gain acceptance of the goals implied by the concept of cultural pluralism. The schools, of course, are central in this process. The contributors to this volume take the position that schools must be responsive to diversity and committed to goals consistent with cultural pluralism.

The theme of *Cultural Pluralism* is intimately related to the notion of equality in education, a subject treated in another volume in the current series on "Contemporary Educational Issues." That volume, *Rethinking Educational Equality*, edited by Andrew T. Kopan and Herbert J. Walberg, explores this much discussed issue from a variety of viewpoints.

Other titles in the current series are:
Crucial Issues in Testing, edited by Ralph W. Tyler and Richard M. Wolf;

Conflicting Conceptions of Curriculum, edited by Elliot Eisner and Elizabeth Vallance.

With this new set of four volumes, the National Society for the Study of Education continues a program begun in 1971 designed to bring out timely books that provide a background for informed discussion of critical issues in education. The Society is greatly indebted to Edgar Epps and his associates for this stimulating and provocative collection of essays.

Kenneth J. Rehage

for the Committee on the Expanded
Publication Program of the
National Society for the Study
of Education

Contributors

Edward J. Barnes, Associate Dean, College of Arts and Sciences, and Director, University-Community Educational Program, University of Pittsburgh; Human Rights Advisor to the Director, National Institute of Education

Alfredo Castaneda, Professor of Education and Psychology, Stanford University

Edgar G. Epps, Marshall Field IV Professor of Urban Education, University of Chicago

Judson Hixson, Graduate Student, University of Chicago

Andrew Kopan, Assistant Professor of Education, De Paul University, Chicago

Thomas F. Pettigrew, Professor of Psychology, Harvard University

Barbara Sizemore, Superintendent of Schools, Washington, D. C.

Diana Slaughter, Assistant Professor of Education and Human Development, University of Chicago

Reed Ueda, Graduate Student, University of Chicago

Contents

Introduction

Racially Separate or Together?

Thomas F. Pettigrew

The United States has had an almost perpetual racial crisis for a generation. But the last third of the twentieth century has begun on a new note, a change of rhetoric and a confusion over goals. Widespread rioting is just one expression of this. The nation hesitates: it seems to have lost its confidence that the problem can be solved; it seems unsure as to even the direction in which a solution lies. In too simple terms, yet in the style of the fashionable rhetoric, the question has become: Shall Americans of the future live racially separate or together?

This new mood is best understood when viewed as part of the eventual sweep of recent years. Ever since World War I, when war orders combined with the curtailment of immigration to encourage massive migration to industrial centers, Negro Americans have been undergoing rapid change as a people. The latest products of this dramatic transformation from southern peasant to northern urbanite are the second and third generations of young people born in the North. The most significant fact about this "newest new Negro" is that he is relatively released from the principal social controls recognized by his parents and grandparents, from the restraints of an extended kinship system, a conservative religion, and an acceptance of the inevitability of white supremacy.

Consider the experience of the twenty-year-old Negro in 1971. He was born in 1951; he was only three years old when the Supreme Court ruled against de jure public school segregation; he was only six years old at the time of the disorders over desegregation in Little Rock, Arkansas; he was nine years old when the student-organized sit-ins began at segregated lunch counters throughout the South; he was twelve when the dramatic march on Washington took place and fifteen when the climactic Selma march occurred. He has witnessed during his short life the initial dismantling of the formal structure of white supremacy. Conventional wisdom holds that such an experience should lead to a highly satisfied generation of young black Americans, but newspaper headlines and social-psychological theory tell us that precisely the opposite is closer to the truth. . . .

The young black surveys the current scene and observes correctly that the benefits of recent racial advances have disproportionately accrued to the expanding middle class, leaving the urban lower class ever further behind. While the middle-class segment of Negro America has expanded from roughly 5 to 25 percent of the Negroes since 1940,[1] the vast majority of blacks remain poor. The young Negro has been raised on the proposition that racial integration is the basic solution to racial injustice, but his doubts grow as opportunities open for the skilled while the daily lives of the unskilled go largely unaffected. Accustomed to a rapid pace of events, many Negro young people wonder if integration will ever be possible in an America where the depth of white resistance to racial change becomes painfully more evident: in 1964, the equivocation of the Democratic Party Convention when faced with the challenge of the Mississippi Freedom Democratic Party; in 1965, the brutality at the bridge in Selma; in 1966, the summary rejection by Congress of antidiscrimination legislation for housing; in 1968, the wanton assassinations within ten weeks of two leading symbols of the integration movement; and, finally, the retrogression in federal action for civil rights under the Nixon administration. These events create understandable doubts as to whether Dr. Martin Luther King's dream of equality can ever be achieved.

It is tempting to project this process further, as many analyses in the mass media unhesitantly have done, and suggest that all of black

America has undergone this vast disillusionment, that blacks now overwhelmingly reject racial integration and are instead turning to separatist goals. As we shall note shortly when reviewing evidence from surveys, this is not the case. Strictly separatist solutions for the black ghettos of urban America have been most elaborately and enthusiastically advanced not by Negro writers but by such popular white writers as the newspaper columnist Joseph Alsop and William H. Ferry, formerly of the Center for the Study of Democratic Institutions.[2] These white analysts, like many white spokesmen for three centuries before them, are prepared to abandon the American dream of equality as it should apply to blacks, in the name of "hard realities" and under a conveniently mistaken notion that separatism is what blacks want anyway.

Yet the militant stance and rhetoric have shifted in recent years. In a real sense, integration has not failed in America, for it still remains to be tried as a national policy. Many Negroes of all ages sense this; they feel that the nation has failed integration rather than that integration has failed the nation. Influential black opinion turned in the late 1960's from integration as the primary goal to other goals—group power, culture, identity, integrity, and pride. Only a relatively small segment of blacks see these new goals as conflicting with integration, but this segment and their assumptions are one focus of this chapter, for they play a disproportionately critical role for the two chief concerns of this volume—racial integration and white racism. The principal contention throughout this book has been that *integration is a necessary condition for the eradication of white racism at both the individual and institutional levels.* But no treatment of this thesis in America of the 1970's would be complete unless it included a brief discussion of this new black mood and its apparently separatist fringe.

Even much of this fringe of young ideological blacks should be described as "apparently" separatist, for the labels that make sense for white Americans necessarily must shift meaning when applied to black Americans. Given the national events that have occurred in their short lives, it is not surprising that this fringe regard racial integration less as an evil than as irrelevant to their preoccupations. They often call for *selective* separatism of one or more aspects of their lives while also demanding their rights of entry into the society's principal institutions. It is no accident that the most outspoken

members of this faction are college students in prestigious and predominantly white universities.

Through the eyes of some whites, this behavior seems highly in-
consistent; it looks as though they talk separation and act integration. But actually the inconsistency is often, though not always,
more apparent than real. Consistent with the new emphasis upon
power and pride, these young blacks are attempting to define their
situation for themselves with particular attention to group autonomy. They are generally as opposed to forced separatism as were
Negroes of past generations, and they reject other imposed doctrines
as well. And for many of them, integration appears to be imposed by
white liberals. "Why is it that you white liberals only insist on *racial*
integration," they often ask, "when separation by class and ethnicity
is a widespread fact of American life? Why is it no one gets upset by
Italian separatism or Jewish separatism, only black separatism?" That
the imposed separation of Negroes in America is qualitatively different and more vast than that practiced against or by any other
sizable American minority, that integration as a doctrine was a creation not of white liberals but of their own fathers and grandfathers—
these answers to the young blacks' insistent questions are intellec-
tually sound. But such responses do not relate to the feelings underlying the question, for they ignore the positive functions of the new
emphasis which excite many young black Americans today.

The positive functions of the new militancy and ideology are ex-
citing precisely because they go to the heart of many young blacks'
personal feelings. If the new ideology's analysis of power at the
societal level is incomplete, its analysis of racial self-hate at the individual level is right on the mark. Its attention to positive identity and
"black is beautiful" is needed and important. Indeed, the abrupt
shift from "Negro" to "black" is an integral part of this movement.
Many members of older generations would have taken offense at
being called "black"; it was considered a slur. But in facing the issue
squarely, young blacks want to be called by the previously forbidden
term in order to externalize the matter and convert it into a positive
label. The fact that the historical justification sometimes cited for
the shift is thin at best is not the point.[3] The important consideration is psychological, and on this ground there is every reason to
believe that the change is healthy.

But the point often overlooked about this new movement is that its cultural and psychological aspects do not require racial separatism. At the close of this chapter, we shall review evidence indicating that this fact is clearly perceived by the great majority of black Americans, who want racial pride and integrity together with integration. Not only is there no necessary contradiction between these two goals, but, once established, group pride is developed best in heterogeneous settings which allow for both individual and group autonomy.

Racial integration has shifted, then, in much black thought from the status of a principal goal to that of one among other mechanisms for achieving "liberation." "Liberation," in its broadest meaning for American race relations, means the total elimination of racial oppression. Similar to the older usage of "freedom," "liberation" means the eradication of the burden of racism that black Americans have borne individually and collectively since 1621. From this particular black perspective, "racially separate or together" is not the issue so much as what mix of strategies and efforts can actually achieve liberation. This view predominated in the August 1970 issue of *Ebony,* which was completely devoted to the topic: "Which Way Black America? Separation? Integration? Liberation?" *Ebony*'s Senior Editor, Lerone Bennett, Jr., puts it forth bluntly:

... The fundamental issue is not separation or integration but liberation. The either/or question of integration or separation does not speak to that proposition; for if our goal is liberation it may be necessary to do both or neither.[4]

We shall return to this point shortly, and we will note that, when the much-abused term "integration" is adequately defined, the position advocated throughout this volume resembles Bennett's in all but rhetoric.

There are, then, positive functions internal to black communities and individuals which this new stance and line of thought appear to have. Much of the present writing in race relations is devoted to these positive functions. But what do these trends spell for the possibility of effectively combating white racism? While accepting the conclusion of the Kerner Commission that this is the basic problem, some recent black thought takes the position that wholly *black* concerns must take such precedence that the fight against white racism is, if not irrelevant, at least of secondary importance. Worse, some elements of the separatist fringe actively contribute to the growth and legitimacy of white racism. Hence, when Roy Innis, the national chairman of the Congress of Racial Equality (CORE), goes on a publicized tour to meet governors of the Deep South in order to advocate his program of separate-but-equal public schools, it hardly helps the effort to eliminate white racism.

This truly separatist fringe, then, is neither necessary to nor typical of the new black thrust. It gains its importance from, and becomes potentially dangerous because of, the way it nourishes white racism at both the individual and institutional levels. And it is for this reason that we need to compare it with white segregationist thought. Obviously, the two groups of separatists have sharply different sources of motivation: the blacks to withdraw; the whites to maintain racial supremacy. Nor are their assumptions on a par for destructive potential. But the danger is that black and white separatism could congeal as movements in the 1970's and help perpetuate a racially separate and racist nation. Because of this danger, it is well to examine the basic assumptions of both groups.

Separatist Assumptions

White segregationists, both in the North and in the South, base their position upon three bedrock assumptions. *Assumption 1* is that separation benefits both races because each feels awkward and uncomfortable with the other: *Whites and Negroes are happiest and most relaxed when in the company of "their own kind."*[5]

Assumption 2 is blatantly racist: *Negroes are inherently inferior to whites, and this is the underlying reality of all racial problems.* The findings of both social and biological science place in serious jeopardy every argument put forward for this assumption, and a decreasing minority of white Americans subscribe to it.[6] Yet it remains the essential substratum of the thinking of white segregationists; racial contact must be avoided, according to this reasoning, if standards of whites are not to be lowered. Thus, attendance at a desegregated school may benefit black children, but it is deemed by segregationists to be inevitably harmful to white children.[7]

Assumption 3 is derived from this assumption of white superiority: *Since contact can never be mutually beneficial, it will inevitably lead to racial conflict.* The White Citizens' Councils in the Deep South, for example, insist that they are opposed to violence and favor racial separation as the primary means of maintaining racial harmony. As long as Negroes "know their place," as long as white supremacy remains unchallenged, strife will be at a minimum.

Black separatists base their position upon three somewhat parallel assumptions. They agree with Assumption 1, that both whites and Negroes are more at ease when separated from each other. It is a harsh fact that blacks have borne the heavier burden of desegregation and have entered previously all-white institutions where open hostility is sometimes practiced by segregationist whites in order to discourage the process, and this is a partial explanation of agreement among blacks with Assumption 1. Yet some of this agreement stems from more subtle situations: the demands by some black student organizations on interracial campuses for all-black facilities have been predicated on this same assumption.

A second assumption of black separatists focuses directly upon white racism. Supported by the chief conclusion of the National Advisory Commission on Civil Disorders, black separatists consider that white racism is the central problem, and that "white liberals" should confine their energies to eradicating it.[8] Let us call this *Assumption 4: White liberals must eradicate white racism.* This assumption underlies two further contentions: namely, that "white liberals" should stay out of the ghetto except as their money and expertise are explicitly requested, and that it is no longer the job of black militants to confront and absorb the abuse of white racists.

The third assumption of black separatists is the most basic of all, and is in tacit agreement with the segregationist notion that interracial contact as it now occurs makes only for conflict. Interaction between black and white Americans, it is held, can never be truly equal and mutually beneficial until blacks first gain personal and group autonomy, self-respect, and power. This makes *Assumption 5: Autonomy is necessary before contact.* It often underlies a two-step theory of how to achieve meaningful integration: the first step requires separation so that Negroes can regroup, unify, and gain a positive self-image and identity; only when this is achieved can the second step, real integration, take place. Ron Karenga, a black leader in Los Angeles, states the idea forcefully: "We're not for isolation, but interdependence. But we can't become interdependent unless we have something to offer. We can live with whites interdependently once we have black power."[9]

Each of these ideological assumptions deserves examination in the light of social-psychological theory and findings.

Social-Psychological Considerations of Separatist Assumptions

Assumption 1: Whites and Negroes Are More Comfortable Apart than Together

There can be no denying that many black and white Americans initially feel uncomfortable and ill at ease when they encounter each other in new situations. This reality is so vivid and so generally recognized that both black and white separatists use it widely in their thinking, though they do not analyze the nature and origins of the situation.

The literature of social science is replete with examples of the phenomenon. Irwin Katz has described the initial awkwardness in biracial task groups in the laboratory: white partners usually assumed an aggressive, imperious role; black partners, a passive role. Similarly, Yarrow found initial tension and keen sensitivity among many Negro children in an interracial summer camp, much of which centered on fears that they would be rejected by white campers.[10] But, more important, such tension does not continue to pervade a truly integrated situation. Katz noted that once blacks were cast in assertive roles, behavior in his small groups became more equalitarian, and this improvement generalized to new situations. Yarrow, too, observed a sharp decline in anxiety and sensitivity among the black children after two weeks of successful integration at the summer camp. As was discussed previously, similar increments in cross-racial acceptance and reductions in tension have been noted in new interracial situations in department stores,[11] the Merchant Marine,[12] the armed forces,[13] and public housing,[14] and even among the Philadelphia police.[15]

This is not to say that new interracial situations invariably lead to acceptance. As we have seen, the *conditions* of the interracial contact are crucial; and even under optimal conditions, the cross-racial acceptance generated by contact is typically limited to the particular situation which created it. A segregated society restricts the generalization effects of even truly integrated situations, and at times like the present, when race assumes such overwhelming salience, the racial tension of the larger society may even poison previously successful interracial settings.

Acquaintance and similarity theory helps to clarify the underlying process. Newcomb states the fundamental tenet as follows:

Insofar as persons have similar attitudes toward things of importance to both or all of them, and discover that this is so, they have shared attitudes; under most conditions the experience of sharing such attitudes is rewarding, and thus provides a basis for mutual attraction.[16]

Rokeach has applied these notions to race relations in the United States with some surprising results. He maintains that rejection of black Americans by white Americans is motivated less by racism than by assumed differences in beliefs and values. In other words, whites generally perceive Negroes as holding beliefs contrasting with their own, and it is this perception—not race per se—that leads to rejection. Indeed, a variety of subjects have supported Rokeach's ideas by typically accepting in a social situation a Negro with beliefs similar to their own over a white with different beliefs.[17]

Additional work has specified the phenomenon more precisely. Triandis and Davis have shown that the relative importance of belief and race in attraction is a joint function of personality and the interpersonal realm in question. Similarity of beliefs is most critical in more formal matters of general personal evaluation and social acceptance, where racial norms are ambiguously defined. Race is most critical in intimate matters of marriage and neighborhood, where racial norms are explicitly defined. For interpersonal realms of an intermediate degree of intimacy, such as friendship, both beliefs and race appear important. There are wide individual differences in the application of these concerns, however, especially in areas where the degree of intimacy is intermediate.[18]

Seen in the light of this work, racial isolation has two negative effects, both of which operate to make optimal interracial contact difficult to achieve and initially tense. First, isolation prevents each group from learning of the beliefs and values they do in fact share. Consequently, Negroes and whites kept apart come to view each other as very different; this belief, combined with racial considerations, causes each race to reject contact with the other. Second, isolation leads in time to the evolution of genuine differences in beliefs and values, making interracial contact in the future even less likely.[19]

A number of findings of social-psychological research support this extrapolation of interpersonal-attraction theory. Stein *et al.* noted that relatively racially isolated white ninth graders in California assumed an undescribed Negro teen-ager to be similar to a Negro teenager who was described as being quite different from themselves.[20] Smith *et al.* found that similarity of beliefs was more critical than racial similarity in desegregated settings, less critical in segregated settings.[21] And the U. S. Commission on Civil Rights, in its study of *Racial Isolation in the Public Schools,* found that both black and white adults who as children had attended interracial schools were more likely as adults to live in an interracial neighborhood and hold more positive racial attitudes than comparable adults who had known only segregated schools.[22] Or, to put it negatively, Americans of both races who experienced only segregated education are more likely to reflect separatist behavior and attitudes as adults.

Racial separatism, then, is a cumulative process. It feeds upon itself and leads its victims to prefer continued separation. In an open-choice situation in Louisville, Kentucky, black children were far more likely to select predominantly white high schools if they were currently attending predominantly white junior high schools.[23] From these data, the U. S. Commission on Civil Rights concluded: "The inference is strong that Negro high school students prefer biracial education only if they have experienced it before. If a Negro student has not received his formative education in biracial schools, the chances are he will not choose to enter one in his more mature school years."[24] Similarly, Negroes who attended segregated schools, the Civil Rights Commission finds, are more likely to believe as adults that interracial schools "create hardships for Negro children" and are less likely to send their children to desegregated schools than are Negroes who attended biracial schools.[25] Note that those who most fear discomfort in biracial settings are precisely those who have experienced such situations least. If desegregation actually resulted in perpetual and debilitating tension, as separatists are so quick to assume, it seems unlikely that children already in the situation would willingly opt for more, or that adults who have had considerable interracial contact as children would willingly submit themselves to biracial neighborhoods and their children to biracial schools.

Moreover, in dealing with the fact that some tension does exist, a social-cost analysis is needed. The question becomes: What price comfort? Racially homogeneous settings are often more comfortable for members of both races, though, as we have just noted, this seems to be most true at the start of the contact and does not seem to be so debilitating that those in the situation typically wish to return to segregated living. But those who remain in racial isolation, both black and white, find themselves increasingly less equipped to compete in an interracial world. Lobotomized patients are more comfortable, too, but they are impaired for life.

Moreover, there is nothing inevitable about the tension that characterizes many initial interracial encounters in the United States. Rather, tension is the direct result of the racial separation that has traditionally characterized our society. In short, separation is the cause of awkwardness in interracial contacts, not the remedy for it.

Assumption 2: Negroes Are Inferior; and
Assumption 4: White Liberals Must Eradicate White Racism

These two assumptions, though of vastly different significance, raise related issues, and both also are classic cases of self-fulfilling prophecies. Treat a people as inferior, force them to play subservient roles,[26] keep them essentially separate, and eventually the people produced by this must come to support the initial racist notions. Likewise, assume that whites are unalterably racist, curtail efforts by Negroes to confront racism directly, separate Negroes from whites even further, and the result will surely be a continuation, if not a heightening, of racism.

The core of racist attitudes, the assumption of innate racial inferiority, has been under sharp attack from social science for over three decades.[27] Partly because of this work, attitudes of white Americans have undergone massive change over these years. Yet a sizable minority of white Americans, perhaps still as large as a fifth of the adult population, persists in harboring racist attitudes in their most vulgar and naïve form. This is an important fact in a time of polarization, such as the present, for this minority becomes the vocal right anchor in the nation's process of social judgment. Racist assumptions not only are nourished by separatism, but in turn rationalize separatism. Equal-status contact is avoided because of the racist stigma placed on black Americans by three centuries of slavery and segregation. But changes are evident both here and in social-distance attitudes. . . . [B]etween 1942 and 1963 the percentage of white Americans who favored racially desegregated schools rose from 30 to 63; the percentage of those with no objections to a Negro neighbor rose from 35 to 63.[28] And . . . this trend did not abate during the mid-1960's of increasing white polarization mistakenly labeled "white backlash." This trend slowed, however, at the very close of the 1960's and in the early 1970's—possibly as a result of less insistence for integration.

The slow but steady erosion of racist and separatist attitudes among white Americans occurred during years of confrontation and change, although the process has been too slow to keep pace with the Negro's rising aspirations for full justice and complete eradication of racism. In a period of confrontation, dramatic events can stimulate surprisingly sharp changes in a short period of time.[29] Consider the attitudes of white Texans before and after the assassination of Martin Luther King, Jr., the riots that followed his murder, and the issuance of the forthright Report of the National Advisory Commission on Civil Disorders.[30] Table 1 shows the data collected before the assassination (in November 1967 and February 1968) and after the assassination (in May 1968 and August 1968). Observe that there were especially large changes in the four areas of relatively formal contact —desegregation in buses, jobs, restaurants, and hotels. In areas of relatively informal contact—desegregation of schools and churches— there was moderate change. And in areas of intimate contact—desegregation of social gatherings, housing, swimming pools, house parties, and college dormitories—there was no significant change. Despite the ceiling effect,[31] approval increased most for those items already most approved. One is reminded of Triandis and Davis' breakdown of racial realms by degree of intimacy.[32] The changes in attitudes also varied among different types of white Texans; the young and the middle class shifted positively the most, again despite ceiling effects.[33] The tentative generalization growing out of these data is that, in times of confrontation, dramatic events can achieve positive attitude changes among those whites and in those areas least subject to separatist norms.

The most solid social-psychological evidence about changes in racial attitudes comes from the studies of contact. . . . Repeated research in a variety of newly desegregated situations showed that the attitudes of whites and blacks toward each other markedly improved:

Table 1. Percent of white Texans who approve

Area of desegregation	Nov. 1967	Feb. 1968	May 1968	Aug. 1968	$\dfrac{\text{May} + \text{Aug.}}{2} - \dfrac{\text{Nov.} + \text{Feb.}}{2}$ Raw change
Formal contact					
Same buses	62.9	64.5	74.3	69.7	+8.3
Same jobs	66.8	69.1	76.1	76.4	+8.2
Same restaurants	57.9	59.9	66.8	66.4	+7.7
Same hotels	53.0	53.8	60.2	59.6	+6.5
Informal contact					
Same schools	53.7	57.6	61.4	61.7	+5.8
Same churches	57.4	60.0	62.5	65.4	+5.2
Teach your child	49.4	51.2	54.3	55.6	+4.7
Intimate contact					
Same social gatherings	39.3	38.9	41.8	44.2	+3.9
Live next door	29.5	32.1	32.0	36.6	+3.5
Same swimming pools	30.9	27.1	29.5	34.6	+3.1
Same house party	26.2	26.2	26.5	29.0	+1.5
College roommate of your child	17.4	17.8	17.1	18.0	0.0

Source: These results are taken from R. T. Riley and T. F. Pettigrew, "Dramatic Events and Racial Attitude Change" (unpublished paper, Harvard University, August 1970). The data are from probability samples of white Texans drawn and interviewed by Belden Associates of Dallas, Texas.

in department stores, public housing,[34] the armed services,[35] and the Merchant Marine,[36] and among government workers,[37] the police,[38] students,[39] and general small-town populations.[40] Some of these findings can be interpreted not as results of contact, but as an indication that more tolerant white Americans seek contact with Negro Americans. A number of the investigations, however, restrict this self-selection factor, making the effects of the new contact itself the only explanation of the significant alterations in attitudes and behavior.

Surveys bear out these findings on a national scale. Hyman and Sheatsley found that among whites the most extensive changes in racial attitudes have occurred where extensive desegregation of public facilities had already taken place.[41] Recall, too, that data from the Coleman Report indicate that white students who attend public schools with blacks are the least likely to prefer all-white classrooms and all-white "close friends"; and this effect is strongest among those who began their interracial schooling in the early grades.[42] This fits neatly with the findings of the U. S. Commission on Civil Rights for both black and white adults who had attended biracial schools as children.[43]

Not all intergroup contact, of course, leads to increased acceptance; sometimes it only makes matters worse. Keep in mind Allport's criteria: prejudice is lessened when the two groups (1) possess equal status in the situation, (2) seek common goals, (3) are cooperatively dependent upon each other, and (4) interact with the positive support of authorities, laws, or customs.[44] These criteria are actually an application of the broader theory of interpersonal attraction. All four conditions maximize the likelihood that shared values and beliefs will be evinced and mutually perceived. Rokeach's belief-similarity factor is, then, apparently important in the effects of optimal contact. Following Triandis and Davis' findings,[45] we would anticipate that alterations in attitudes achieved by intergroup contact, at least initially, will be greatest in formal areas and least in intimate areas—as was true of the changes in attitudes of white Texans brought about by dramatic events in the early spring of 1968.

From this social-psychological perspective, the assumption of black separatists that "white liberals" should eliminate white racism seems to be an impossible and quixotic hope. One can readily appreciate the militants' desire to avoid further abuse from white racists, but their model for change is woefully inadequate. White liberals can attack racist attitudes publicly, conduct research on racist assertions, set the stage for confrontation. But with all the will in the world they cannot accomplish by themselves the needed push, the dramatic events, the actual interracial contact which have gnawed away at racist beliefs for a generation. A century ago the fiery and perceptive Frederick Douglass phrased the issue pointedly:

I have found in my experience that the way to break down an unreasonable custom is to contradict it in practice. To be sure in pursuing this course I have had to contend not merely with the white race but with the black. The one has condemned me for my presumption in daring to associate with it and the other for pushing myself where it takes it for granted I am not wanted.[46]

Assumption 3: Contact Must Lead to Conflict; and
Assumption 5: Autonomy Is Needed before Contact

History reveals that white separatists are correct when they contend that racial change creates conflict, that if only the traditions of white supremacy were to go unchallenged racial harmony might be restore   One of the quietest periods in American racial history, 1895-1915, witnessed the construction of the massive system of institutional racism as it is known today—the "nadir of Negro American history," as Rayford Logan calls it.[47] The price of those two decades of relative peace is still being paid by the nation. Even if it were possible now to gain racial calm by inaction, the United States could not afford the enormous cost.

But if inaction is clearly impossible, the types of action necessary are not so clear. Black separatists believe that efforts to further interracial contact should be abandoned or at least delayed until greater personal and group autonomy is achieved by Negroes. This view and the attitudes of white separatists just mentioned are two sides of the same coin. Both leave the struggle against racism in attitudes completely in the hands of "white liberals." And the two assumptions run a similar danger. Racism is reflected not only in attitudes but, more importantly, in institutionalized arrangements that operate to restrict the choices open to blacks. Both forms of racism are fostered by segregation, and both have to be confronted directly by Negroes. To withdraw into the ghetto, psychologically tempting as this may be for many, is essentially to give up the fight to alter the racially discriminatory operations of the nation's chief institutions. The Rev.

Jesse L. Jackson, the Chicago black leader of Operation Breadbasket, makes the same point in forceful terms:

> Let's use this analogy. Assuming that racism is a hot fire. If we're gonna take over things and run them and destroy racism; we got to get to the core of the fire. You can't destroy it by running away from it. The fact is, at this point in American history, racism is in trouble in terms of the government, economy, political order and even the psychological order.[48]

The issues involved are shown schematically in Figure 1. By varying contact—separation and an ideologically vague concept of "autonomy," four cells may be set up that represent the various possibilities under discussion. Cell A, true integration, refers to institutionalized biracial situations where there is cross-racial friendship, racial

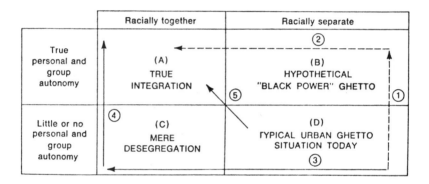

Figure 1. Schematic diagram of autonomy and contact-separation. Dotted lines denote hypothetical paths; solid lines, actual paths.*

interdependence, and a strong measure of personal and group autonomy. Such situations do exist in America today, but they are rare islands in a sea of conflict. Cell B represents the autonomous ghetto postulated by advocates of black separatism, relatively independent of the larger society and far more viable than is commonly the case now. This is an ideologically derived hypothetical situation, for no such urban ghettos exist today. Cell C stands for merely desegregated

---

*The author is indebted to Professor Karl Deutsch of Harvard University for several stimulating conversations out of which came this diagram.

situations. These are often mistakenly called "integrated." They are institutionalized biracial settings which involve little cross-racial acceptance and, often, patronizing legacies of white supremacy. Cell D represents today's typical highly separate urban ghetto with little or no personal or group autonomy.

Definitional confusions may obscure the meaning of Figure 1, especially the definition of "integration." This term became almost a hallowed symbol of the civil rights movement of previous decades, and its present disparagement in newer black thought may be traced in part to this fact. But most disparagement of "integration" is due to definitional confusion between it and "assimilation" and between it and desegregation as diagramed in Figure 1. As Lerone Bennett rightly points out, these confusions among both whites and blacks stem from employing exclusively a white standard of reference:

One of the greatest enemies of integration in America today is the word integration. Contary to the hopes of some and the fears of others, integration does not mean black elimination. Integration may or may not lead to assimilation, but assimilation does not necessarily mean the disappearance of a minority. . . . [D]ifferences can be eliminated in favor of a creative minority. Both "integrationists" and "separatists" forget that there is a blackening process as well as a whitening process. Liberationists, who recognize this dialectic, say blacks must assimilate and not be assimilated. . . . Integration is not disappearance; nor is it simple contiguity . . . since men have given the word integration a bad name, we shall use the word *transformation* to refer to the real thing.[49]

Cell A refers to "the real thing," to the integration of *whites* as well as blacks, to the end product of Lerone Bennett's "transformation."

Except for white separatists, observers of diverse persuasions agree that the achievement of true integration (cell A) should be the ultimate goal. But there are, crudely speaking, three contrasting ways of getting there from the typical current situation (cell D). The black separatist assumes that only one route is possible: from the depressed ghetto of today to the hypothetical ghetto of tomorrow and then, perhaps, on to true integration (lines 1 and 2 in Figure 1). The desegregationist assumes precisely the opposite route: from the present-day ghetto to mere desegregation and then, hopefully, on to true integration (lines 3 and 4 in Figure 1). But there is a third, more direct route, right across from the current ghetto to true integration (line 5 in Figure 1). Experience to date combines with a number of

social-psychological considerations to favor the last of these possibilities with some important qualifications.

The route favored by black separatists has a surprising appeal for
an untested theory; besides those whites who welcome any alternative to integration, it seems to appeal to militant black leaders search-
ing for a new direction into which to channel the ghetto's rage, and
to blacks who just wish to withdraw as far away from whites as
possible. Yet, on reflection, it can be seen that the argument involves
the perverse notion that the way to bring two groups together is to
separate them further. One is reminded of the detrimental consequences of isolation in economics, through "closed markets," and in
genetics, through "genetic drift." In social psychology, isolation between two contiguous groups generally leads to: (1) the development
of diverse values, (2) reduced intergroup communication, (3) uncor-
rected perceptual distortions of each other, and (4) the growth of
vested interests within both groups for continued separation. Race
relations in the United States already suffer from each of these conditions, and the proposal for further separation, even if a gilded
ghetto were possible, can only exacerbate them.

In fairness, it should be emphasized again that the criticisms here
are directed against the concept of the insulated ghetto, not the
shrewder and more subtle notions of power and regrouping combined with challenges to the restriction of choice imposed by the
nation's leading institutions. As was mentioned at the beginning of
this chapter, a much larger segment of militant blacks, judging from
their actions, adheres to the latter program. The fascinations of the
more romantic notions of a totally self-sufficient black community
and even occasional expressions of black chauvinism are apparently
diminished by many of the unromantic facts of the situation.

We will not pursue the many economic and political difficulties
inherent in the concept of the insulated ghetto, but it should be
mentioned that the resources immediately available in the ghetto for
the task are meager. Recognizing this limitation, black separatists call
for massive federal aid with no strings attached. But this requires a
national consensus. Some separatists consider that the direct path to
integration (line 5 in Figure 1) is idealistic dreaming, then turn and
assume that the same racist society that resists integration will un-
hesitatingly pour a significant portion of its treasure into the ghetto.
"Local control" without access to the necessary tax base is not con-

trol. This raises the question of the political limitations of this route. Irish-Americans entered the mainstream through the political system, and this method is often cited as appropriate to black separatism—but is it really? Faster than any other immigrant group except Jewish-Americans, the Irish have assimilated on the direct route of Figure 1. Forced to remain in ghettos at first, the Irish did not settle for "local control" but strove to win city hall itself. Boston's legendary James Michael Curley won "Irish power" not by becoming mayor of the South Boston ghetto, but by becoming mayor of the entire city. Analogies between immigrants and blacks contain serious inaccuracies, however, since immigrants never suffered from slavery and legalized segregation. But to the extent an analogy is appropriate, Mayor Carl Stokes of Cleveland, Mayor Richard Hatcher of Gary, and Mayor Kenneth Gibson of Newark are far closer to the Irish-American model than are black separatists.

A critical part of the thinking of black separatists centers on the psychological concept of "fate control"—more familiar to psychologists as Rotter's internal control of reinforcement variable.[50] "Until we control our own destinies, our own schools and areas," goes the argument, "blacks cannot possibly achieve the vital sense of fate control." Data from the Coleman Report are cited to show that fate control is a critical correlate of achievement in school for black children.[51] But no mention is made of the additional fact that levels of fate control among black children were found by Coleman to be significantly higher in interracial schools than in all-Negro schools. Black separatists brush this important finding aside because all-Negro schools today are not what they envision for the future. Yet the fact remains that interracial schools appear to be facilitating the growth of fate control among Negro students now; the ideological contention that fate control can be developed as well or better in uniracial schools remains an untested and hypothetical assertion.

Despite the problems, black separatists feel that their route (lines 1 and 2 in Figure 1) is the only way to true integration, in part because they regard the indirect route of desegregation (lines 3 and 4) as an affront to their dignity. Anyone familiar with the blatantly hostile and subtly rejecting acts that typify some interracial situations will understand this repudiation of nonautonomous desegregation (cell C).[52] The U. S. Commission on Civil Rights, in reanalyzing Coleman's data, found that this provided the tool for distinguishing empirically between effective and ineffective biracial schools where whites form the majority. Achievement, college aspirations, and the sense of fate control by Negro students proved to be highest in truly integrated schools when these schools are independently defined as biracial institutions characterized by no racial tension and wide-spread cross-racial friendship. Merely desegregated schools, defined as biracial institutions typified by racial tension and little cross-racial friendship, have scant benefits over segregated schools.[53]

This finding reflects Allport's conditions for optimal contact. Truly integrated institutions afford the type of contact that maximizes cross-racial acceptance and the similarity of beliefs described by Rokeach.[54] They apparently also maximize the positive and minimize the negative factors which Katz has isolated as important for performance of Negroes in biracial task groups.[55] And they also seem to increase the opportunity for beneficial cross-racial evaluations, which may well be critical mediators of the effects of biracial schools.[56] Experimental research following up these leads is now called for to detail the precise social-psychological processes operating in the truly integrated situation.[57]

The desegregation route (lines 3 and 4 in Figure 1) has been successfully navigated, though the contention of black separatists that Negroes bear the principal burden for this effort is undoubtedly true. Southern institutions that have attained integration, for example, have typically traveled this indirect path. This route, then, is not as hypothetical as the route advocated by black separatists, but it is hardly to be preferred over the route of direct integration (line 5).

Why not the direct route, then? The standard answer is that it is impossible, that demographic trends and resistance from whites make it out of the question in our time. One is reminded of the defenders of slavery in the 1850's, who attacked the Abolitionists as unrealistic dreamers and insisted that slavery was so deeply entrenched that efforts should be limited to making it into a benign institution. If the nation acts on such speculations, of course, they will probably be proven correct. What better way is there to prevent racial change than to act on the assumption that it is impossible?

The belief that integration is impossible, however, is based on some harsh facts of urban racial demography. Between 1950 and 1960, the average annual increment of Negro population in the central cities of the United States was 320,000; from 1960 to 1966 the estimated annual growth climbed to 400,000, though reduced in-migration from the rural South has lowered this annual growth rate considerably since 1966.[58] In the suburbs, however, the average annual growth of the Negro population declined from 60,000 between 1950 and 1960 to an estimated 33,000 between 1960 and 1966, though it has sharply increased since 1966.[59] In other words, it would require several times the present trend in growth of Negro populations in the suburbs just to maintain the sprawling central-city ghettos at their present size. In the nation's largest metropolitan areas, then, the trend is still pushing in the direction of ever-increasing separatism.

But these bleak data are not the whole picture. In the first place, they refer especially to the very largest of the metropolitan areas—to New York City, Chicago, Los Angeles, Philadelphia, Detroit, Washington, D.C., and Baltimore. Most Negro Americans do not live in these places, but rather in areas where racial integration is in fact possible in the short run if attempts in good faith are made. There are more Berkeleys—small enough for school integration to be effectively achieved—than there are New York Cities. In the second place, the presumed impossibility of reversing racial trends in the central city are based on antimetropolitan assumptions. We noted repeatedly throughout Part One of this volume that without metropolitan cooperation central cities—and many suburbs, too—will find their racial and other basic problems continuing. Do we need to assume such cooperation impossible? We previously proposed effective state and federal incentives to further this cooperation. Moreover, some large black ghettos are already extending into the suburbs (e.g., east of Pittsburgh and west of Chicago); the first tentative metropolitan schemes to aid racial integration are emerging in a variety of cities (e.g., Boston, Hartford, Rochester, and Portland, Oregon); and several major metropolitan areas have been consolidated (e.g., Miami-Dade County and Nashville-Davidson County). Once the issue is looked at in metropolitan terms, its dimensions become more manageable. Black Americans are found in America's metropolitan areas in almost the same ratio as white Americans: about two-thirds of each group reside in these 212 regions. On a metropolitan basis, therefore, Negroes are not disproportionately metropolitan.

Yet it must be admitted that many young blacks, separatist and otherwise, are simply not convinced by such arguments. Such large-scale proposals as metropolitan educational parks strike them as far-away pipe dreams of no significance to their immediate problems. Contact theory holds little appeal. They rightfully argue that All-port's four conditions do not typify the American national scene. How often, they ask, do blacks actually possess equal status in situations with whites? And in struggles for racial power, as they view it, can there be a cooperative seeking of common goals? And as for the possibility that true integration of cell A will be sanctioned by those in authority, they say ruefully, consider the public images on racial matters of Nixon, Mitchell, Agnew, Carswell. Maybe the demographic arguments against the possibility of integration are overdrawn, they concede, but can one realistically expect Allport's conditions of positive contact to become the rule in the foreseeable future of the United States?

Underlying this criticism is less a theoretical and ideological difference than a sharply contrasting assessment of the probabilities and possibilities of America's race relations. These black spokesmen may well be right. The United States may indeed be so racist both as to individuals and structure that the type of institutional changes advocated throughout this volume will never be achieved. No footnoting of references or social-psychological theory can refute this possibility, but I hope it is wrong. The entire analysis of this book is predicated on the more optimistic view that somehow American society will muddle through. To assume otherwise, once again, is to risk contributing to the problem by engaging in a self-fulfilling prophecy.

Moreover, the attack on contact theory is based in part on a misreading of it. *Situations* meeting Allport's four conditions do exist in the United States, and we have seen that they are becoming more numerous in such realms as employment. True, as noted, these truly integrated situations are still isolated islands and together do not constitute a critical mass nationally. Yet the status of Negroes is rising in the United States. Indeed, the personal lives of the black critics themselves typically attest to this social mobility, for roughly 90 percent of middle-class blacks today derive from families which were lower class in 1940. But . . . these very gains create rapidly rising expectations and a keen sense of relative deprivation, some of which gets channeled among some blacks into the separatist ideology under discussion.

Nor are power struggles as completely racial and competitive as critics claim. For one thing, power conflicts almost invariably involve class as well as racial interests, and to the extent that class is involved there are at least potential white allies. White Americans, after all, are an even more diverse assortment than black Americans. Thus, Mayor Carl Stokes received 22 percent of the white vote in Cleveland in November of 1969, Thomas Bradley 40 percent in the Los Angeles mayoralty runoff in June of 1969, Mayor Kenneth Gibson 16 percent in Newark in June of 1970. The percentages are low because of racism, but they do occur and rise over time (Stokes received in general elections only 11 percent in 1965, and 19 percent in 1967). But actually the theory requires only that blacks and some whites share common goals to the point where coalitions become important to both; one of these coalitions is called the Democratic Party, which, since Franklin Roosevelt, has consisted of a precarious combination of minorities which together total a registration far larger than that of the rival party.

Finally, concerning Allport's fourth condition on the sanction of laws and authorities, there is solid evidence in civil rights legislation and other institutional changes that American society is slowly moving toward the sanctioning of true integration. By and large, of course, America's institutions still do not play this role; they are racist, in the Kerner Commission's plain language, in that their normal operations still act typically to restrict choice for blacks. But positive change is evident from the appearance of Negroes on television to their participation in former bastions of white privilege. True, as far as race is concerned the Nixon administration is a throwback to the naïveté of early twentieth-century administrations; it offers no "authority sanction," nor does it promise to in its remaining years. Yet there are other political alternatives which would willingly offer the racial leadership the nation so desperately needs. To opt out of the opposition, to assume that the Mitchells and Agnews are inevitable and typical products of the American political system, is to ensure that such men will in fact remain in power.

To argue for route 5 in Figure 1 is not to assume that it will be easy to achieve, or that Allport's optimal conditions for intergroup contact apply generally throughout America at present. The direct path does stress that *simultaneous* attention must be given to both integration and individual and collective autonomy, for today's cell D has neither and tomorrow's cell A must have both. And neither the desegregation (paths 3 and 4 of Figure 1) nor the separatist (paths 1 and 2) route gives this simultaneous attention. Once again, Bennett phrases the argument cogently:

It is impossible, Simon de Beauvoir said, to draw a straight line in a curved space. Both "integrationists" and "separatists" are trying to create right angles in a situation which only permits curves. The only option is Transformation of a situation which does not permit a clear-cut choice in either direction. This means that we must face the fact that it is impossible to move 30 million African-Americans anywhere.[60]

Implications for Policy

Much of the confusion over policy seems to derive from the assumption that since *complete* integration in the biggest cities will not be possible in the near future, present efforts toward opening opportunities for integration for both Negro and white Americans are premature. This thinking obscures two fundamental issues. First, the democratic objective is not total racial integration and the elimination of black neighborhoods; the idea is simply to provide an honest choice between separation and integration. Today only separation is available; integration is closed to blacks who would choose it. The long-term goal is not a complete obliteration of cultural pluralism, of distinctive Negro areas, but rather the transformation of these ghettos from racial prisons to ethnic areas freely chosen or not chosen. Life within ghettos can never be fully satisfactory as long as there are Negroes who reside within them only because discrimination requires them to.

Second, the integrationist alternative will not become a reality as long as we disparage it or abandon it to future generations. Exclusive attention to programs for enriching life in the ghetto is almost certain, to use Kenneth Clark's pointed word, to "embalm" the ghetto, to seal it in even further from the rest of the nation (making line 2 in Figure 1 even less likely). This danger explains the recent interest of conservative whites in enrichment programs for the ghetto. The bribe is straightforward: "Stop rioting and stop demanding integration, and we'll minimally support separatist programs within the ghetto." Even black separatists are understandably ambivalent about such offers, as they come from sources long identified with opposition to all racial change. Should the bargain be struck, however, race relations in the United States will be dealt still another serious blow.

Yet a policy concentrating exclusively on integration, like one concentrating exclusively on enrichment, runs its own danger of worsening the situation. As many black spokesmen correctly point out, a single-minded pursuit of integration is likely to blind us to the urgent requirements of today's black ghettos. Either policy followed mechanically and exclusively, then, has serious limitations which the rival strategy is designed to correct. This fact strongly suggests that a national transformation from a racist society to an open society will require a judicious mix of both the strategies.

The outlines of the situation, then, are these: (1) Widespread integration is possible everywhere in the United States except in the largest central cities. (2) It will not come unless present trends are reversed and considerable resources are provided for the process. (3) Big central cities will continue to have significant concentrations of Negroes even with successful metropolitan dispersal. (4) Large Negro ghettos are presently in need of intensive enrichment. (5) Some enrichment programs for the ghetto run the clear and present danger of embalming the ghetto further.

Given this situation and the social-psychological considerations we have been discussing throughout this book, the overall strategy needed must contain the following elements:

1. A major effort toward racial integration must be mounted in order to provide genuine choice to all Negro Americans in all realms of life. This effort should envisage complete attainment of the goal in smaller communities and cities by the late 1970's and a halting of separatist trends in major central cities, with a movement toward metropolitan cooperation.

2. A simultaneous effort is required to enrich the vast central-city ghettos of the nation, to change them structurally, and to improve life in them. In order to avoid "embalming" them, however, strict criteria must be applied to proposed enrichment programs to insure that they will not hinder later dispersal and integration. Restructuring the economics of the ghetto, especially by developing urban cooperatives, is a classic example of productive enrichment. Effective job training programs offer another example of productive enrichment. The building of enormous public housing developments within the ghetto presents a good illustration of counterproductive enrichment. Some programs, such as the decentralization of huge public school systems or the encouragement of business ownership by Negroes, can be either productive or counterproductive depending

upon how they are focused. A decentralization plan of many small homogeneous school districts for New York City is clearly counter-productive for later integration; a plan involving a relatively small number of heterogeneous school districts for New York City could well be productive. Likewise, black entrepreneurs who are encouraged to open small shops and are expected to prosper with an all-black clientele are not only part of a counterproductive plan, but are probably commiting economic suicide. Negro businessmen who are encouraged to pool their resources to establish somewhat larger operations, and to appeal to white as well as black customers on major traffic arteries in and out of the ghetto, could be an important part of a productive plan.

In short, a mixed strategy is called for—both integration and en-richment—and it must contain safeguards that the two aspects will not impede each other. Results of recent surveys strongly suggest that such a mixed strategy would meet with widespread approval among black Americans. On the basis of their extensive survey of black residents in fifteen major cities in 1968, Campbell and Schu-man conclude:

Separatism appeals to from five to eighteen per cent of the Negro sample, depending on the question, with the largest appeal involving black ownership of stores and black administration of schools in Negro neighborhoods, and the smallest appeal the rejection of whites as friends or in other informal contacts. Even on questions having the largest appeal, however, more than three-quarters of the Negro sample indicate a clear preference for integration. Moreover, the reasons given by respondents for their choices suggest that the desire for integra-tion is not simply a practical wish for better material facilities, but represents a commitment to principles of nondiscrimination and racial harmony.[61]

Young men prove to be the most forthright separatists, but even here the percentages of men aged sixteen to nineteen who were separatists ranged only from eleven to twenty-eight. An interesting interaction between type of separatism and educational level of the respondent appears in Campbell and Schuman's data. Among the twenty- to thirty-nine-year-olds, college graduates tended to be more separatist in those realms where their training gives them a vested interest in positions free of competition—black-owned stores for black neighborhoods, black teachers in mostly black schools. The poorly educated were most likely to believe that whites should be discouraged from taking part in civil rights organizations and to agree that "Negroes should have nothing to do with whites if they can help it" and that "there should be a separate black nation here."[62]

But if separatism draws little favorable response even in the most politicized ghettos, positive aspects of cultural pluralism attract wide interest. For example, 42 percent endorse the statement that "Negro schoolchildren should study an African language." And this interest seems rather general across age, sex, and education categories. Campbell and Schuman regard this as evidence of a broadly supported attempt "to emphasize black consciousness *without* rejection of whites. . . . A substantial number of Negroes want *both* integration and black identity."[63] Or, in the terms of this chapter, they prefer cell A in Figure 1—"true integration."

When viewed historically, this preferred combination of black consciousness without separation is not a new position for black Americans. It was, for example, their dominant response to the large-scale movement of Marcus Garvey in the 1920's. Garvey, a West Indian, stressed pride in Africa and black beauty and successfully mounted a mass movement throughout the urban ghettos of the day, but his famous "back to Africa" separatist appeals were largely ignored as irrelevant.

Campbell and Schuman's data indicate little if any change from the prointegration results of earlier surveys.[64] And they are consistent with the results of surveys in Detroit, Miami, New York City, and other cities.[65] Data from Bedford-Stuyvesant in Brooklyn are especially significant, for here separatist ideology and a full-scale enrichment program are in full view. Yet when asked if they would prefer to live on a block with people only of the same race or people of every race, 80 percent of the Negro respondents chose an interracial block. Interestingly, the largest Negro segment choosing integration—88 percent—consisted of residents of public housing where a modest amount of interracial tenancy still prevails.[66]

A final study from Watts links these surveys to the analysis of this chapter. Ransford found that willingness of Negroes to use violence was closely and positively related to a sense of powerlessness, feelings of racial dissatisfaction, and limited contact with whites. Respondents who indicated that they had no social contact with white people, "like going to the movies together or visiting each other's homes," were significantly more likely to feel powerless and express racial dissatisfaction as well as to report greater willingness to use violence.[67] The personal, group, and national costs of racial separatism are clearly great.

A Final Word

Racially separate or together? Our social-psychological examination of separatist assumptions leads to the assertion of one imperative: the attainment of a viable, democratic nation, free from personal and institutional racism, requires extensive racial integration in all realms of life as well as vast programs of ghetto enrichment. To prescribe more separation because of discomfort, racism, conflict, or the need for autonomy is like getting drunk again to cure a hangover. The nation's binge of *apartheid* must not be exacerbated but alleviated.

Notes

An earlier draft of this paper was the author's presidential address to the Society for the Psychological Study of Social Issues, delivered at the annual convention of the American Psychological Association in San Francisco, California, on September 1, 1968.

1. These figures derive from three gross estimates of "middle-class" status: annual family income of $6,000 or more, high school graduation, or white-collar occupation. Thus, in 1961 roughly one-fifth of Negro families received in excess of $6,000 (a percentage that now must approach one-fourth, even in constant dollars); in 1960, 22 percent of Negroes over twenty-four years of age had completed high school; and in 1966, 21 percent of employed Negroes held white-collar occupations.

2. Joseph Alsop, "No More Nonsense about Ghetto Education!" *New Republic* 157 (July 22, 1967), 18-23; and "Ghetto Education," *New Republic* 157 (November 18, 1967), 18-23. For answers to these articles, see: R. Schwartz, T. Pettigrew, and M. Smith, "Fake Panaceas for Ghetto Education," *New Republic* 157 (September 23, 1967), 16-19; and "Is Desegregation Impractical?" *New Republic* 157 (January 6, 1968), 27-29; W. H. Ferry, "Black Colonies: A Modest Proposal," *The Center Magazine* 1 (January 1968), 74-76. Ferry even proposes that "black colonies" be formally established in American central cities, complete with treaties enacted with the federal government. The position of black militants is in sharp contrast to this; they complain of having a colonial status now and do not consider it a desirable state of affairs.

3. It is sometimes held that "Negro" was the term for slaves; but actually both "Negro" and "black" were frequently used in documents concerning slaves. Some critics argue that the true skin color of Negro Americans is basically

brown, not black, and that the term "black" is therefore inappropriate. But of course "white" Americans are seldom white either; besides, "Negro" is simply the Spanish word for "black." The importance of the term "black" is in fact basically psychological. I have used both terms interchangeably because surveys indicate each is preferred by different segments of the Negro community.

4. Lerone Bennett, Jr., "Liberation," *Ebony* 25 (August 1970), 36-43.

5. Clairette P. Armstrong and A. J. Gregor, "Integrated Schools and Negro Character Development: Some Considerations of the Possible Effects," *Psychiatry* 27 (February 1964), 69-72.

6. T. F. Pettigrew, *A Profile of the Negro American* (Princeton, N.J.: Van Nostrand, 1964).

7. Analysis specifically directed on this point shows that this contention is not true for predominantly white classrooms as contrasted with comparable all-white classrooms. (United States Commission on Civil Rights, *Racial Isolation in the Public Schools* [Washington, D.C.: U.S. Government Printing Office, 1967], 1, 160.)

8. National Advisory Commission on Civil Disorders, *U.S. Riot Commission Report* (Washington, D.C.: U.S. Government Printing Office, 1968).

9. B. E. Calame, "A West Coast Militant Talks Tough But Helps Avert Racial Trouble," *The Wall Street Journal* 172 (No. 1, July 26, 1968), 15. Karenga's contention that blacks presently have nothing "to offer" a racially interdependent America strangely echoes similar contentions of white racists.

10. Irwin Katz, "Review of Evidence Relating to Effects of Desegregation on the Performance of Negroes," *American Psychologist* 19 (June 1964), 381-99; and M. R. Yarrow (ed.), "Interpersonal Dynamics in a Desegregation Process," *Journal of Social Issues* 14 (No. 1, 1958), 3-63.

11. John Harding and Russell Hogrefe, "Attitudes of White Department Store Employees toward Negro Co-workers," *Journal of Social Issues* 8 (No. 1, 1952), 18-28; and G. Saenger and E. Gilbert, "Customer Reactions to the Integration of Negro Sales Personnel," *International Journal of Opinion and Attitude Research* 4 (Spring 1950), 57-76.

12. I. N. Brophy, "The Luxury of Anti-Negro Prejudice," *Public Opinion Quarterly* 9 (Winter 1946), 456-66.

13. S. A. Stouffer, E. A. Suchman, L. C. DeVinney, S. A. Star, and R. M. Williams, Jr., *Studies in Social Psychology in World War II*, Vol. I, *The American Soldier: Adjustment during Army Life* (Princeton, N.J.: Princeton University Press, 1949).

14. M. Deutsch and M. Collins, *Interracial Housing: A Psychological Evaluation of a Social Experiment* (Minneapolis: University of Minnesota Press, 1951); Marie Jahoda and Patricia West, "Race Relations in Public Housing," *Journal of Social Issues* 7 (Nos. 1 and 2, 1951), 132-39; D. M. Wilner, R. Walkley, and S. W. Cook, *Human Relations in Interracial Housing: A Study of the Contact Hypothesis* (Minneapolis: University of Minnesota Press, 1955); and E. Works, "The Prejudice-Interaction Hypothesis from the Point of View of the Negro Minority Group," *American Journal of Sociology* 67 (July 1961), 47-52.

15. W. M. Kephart, *Racial Factors and Urban Law Enforcement* (Philadelphia: University of Pennsylvania Press, 1957).

16. T. M. Newcomb, R. H. Turner, and P. E. Converse, *Social Psychology: The Study of Human Interaction* (New York: Holt, Rinehart and Winston, 1965).

17. M. Rokeach, P. Smith and R. Evans, "Two Kinds of Prejudice or One?" in M. Rokeach (ed.), *The Open and Closed Mind* (New York: Basic Books, 1960); M. Rokeach and L. Mezei, "Race and Shared Belief as Factors in Social Choice," *Science* 151 (January 14, 1966), 167-72; Carole R. Smith, L. Williams, and R. H. Willis, "Race, Sex and Belief as Determinants of Friendship Acceptance," *Journal of Personality and Social Psychology* 5 (February 1967), 127-37; D. D. Stein, "The Influence of Belief Systems on Interpersonal Preference," *Psychological Monographs* 80 (No. 616, 1966); and D. D. Stein, J. A. Hardyck, and M. B. Smith, "Race and Belief: An Open and Shut Case," *Journal of Personality and Social Psychology* 1 (April 1965), 281-90.

18. H. C. Triandis and E. E. Davis, "Race and Belief as Determinants of Behavioral Intentions," *Journal of Personality and Social Psychology*, 2 (November 1965), 715-25. This resolution of the earlier controversy between Triandis and Rokeach takes on added weight when the data from studies favorable to Rokeach's position are examined carefully. (H. C. Triandis, "A Note on Rokeach's Theory of Prejudice," *Journal of Abnormal and Social Psychology* 62 (January 1961), 184-86; and M. Rokeach, "Belief versus Race as Determinants of Social Distance: Comment on Triandis' Paper," *Journal of Abnormal and Social Psychology* 62 (January 1961), 187-88). That interpersonal realms lead to varying belief-race weightings is borne out by Table 4 in Stein *et al., op cit.*; that intensely prejudiced subjects, particularly in environments where racist norms even extend into less-intimate realms, will act on race primarily is shown by one sample of whites in the Deep South in Smith *et al., op. cit.*

19. Both black and white observers tend to exaggerate racial differences in basic values. Rokeach and Parker note from data from national surveys that, while there appear to be real value differences between the rich and the poor, once socioeconomic factors are controlled there are no sharp value differences between black and white Americans. M. Rokeach and S. Parker, "Values as Social Indicators of Poverty and Race Relations in America," *Annals of the American Academy of Political and Social Science* 388 (March 1970), 97-111.

20. Stein *et al., op. cit.*

21. Smith *et al., op. cit.*

22. United States Commission on Civil Rights, *op. cit.*

23. For twelve junior highs, the Spearman-Brown rank-order correlation between the white junior high percentage and the percentage of Negroes choosing predominantly white high schools is +.82 (corrected for ties)—significant at better than the 1 percent level of confidence.

24. United States Commission on Civil Rights, *Civil Rights USA: Public Schools, Southern States, 1962* (Washington, D.C.: U.S. Government Printing Office, 1963).

25. United States Commission on Civil Rights, *Racial Isolation in the Public Schools.*

26. For a role-analysis interpretation of racial interactions in the United States, see Pettigrew, *op. cit.*

27. One of the first significant efforts in this direction was the classic intelligence study by Otto Klineberg, *Negro Intelligence and Selective Migration* (New York: Columbia University Press, 1935). For a summary of current scientific work relevant to racist claims regarding health, intelligence, and crime, see Pettigrew, *op. cit.*

28. H. H. Hyman and P. B. Sheatsley, "Attitudes toward Desegregation," *Scientific American* 211 (July 1964), 16-23; and P. B. Sheatsley, "White Attitudes toward the Negro," in T. Parsons and K. B. Clark (eds.), *The Negro American* (Boston: Houghton Mifflin, 1966).

29. R. T. Riley and T. F. Pettigrew, "Dramatic Events and Racial Attitude Change" (unpublished paper, Harvard University, August 1970).

30. National Advisory Commission on Civil Disorders, *op. cit.*

31. "The ceiling effect" occurs when initial approval is already so high, so near its "ceiling" of 100 percent, that further gains in approval would not generally be as large as when there is less initial approval.

32. Triandis and Davis, *op. cit.*

33. Similar to these results was an overall shift of approximately 5 percent toward favoring the racial desegregation of public schools noted among white Texans between two surveys taken immediately before and after the 1957 school crisis in Little Rock. And once again, the most positive shifts were noted among the young and the middle class. (Riley and Pettigrew, *op. cit.*)

34. Deutsch and Collins, *op. cit.*; Jahoda and West, *op. cit.*; Wilner *et al.*, *op. cit.*; and Works, *op. cit.*

35. Stouffer *et al.*, *op. cit.*; and B. MacKenzie, "The Importance of Contact in Determining Attitudes toward Negroes," *Journal of Abnormal and Social Psychology* 43 (October 1948), 417-41.

36. Brophy, *op. cit.*

37. MacKenzie, *op. cit.*

38. Kephart, *op. cit.*

39. MacKenzie, *op. cit.*

40. R. M. Williams, Jr., *Strangers Next Door: Ethnic Relations in American Communities* (Englewood Cliffs, N.J.: Prentice-Hall, 1964).

41. Hyman and Sheatsley, *op. cit.* This is, of course, a two-way causal relationship. Not only does desegregation erode racist attitudes, but desegregation tends to come first to areas where white attitudes are least racist to begin with. Hyman and Sheatsley's finding, however, specifically highlights the former phenomenon: "In those parts of the South where some measure of school integration has taken place official action has *preceded* public sentiment, and public sentiment has then attempted to accommodate itself to the new situation."

42. J. S. Coleman, E. Q. Campbell, C. J. Hobson, M. McPartland, A. M. Mood, F. D. Weinfield, and R. L. York, *Equality of Educational Opportunity* (Washington, D.C.: U.S. Government Printing Office, 1966).

43. U.S. Commission on Civil Rights, *Racial Isolation in the Public Schools.*

44. Gordon W. Allport, *The Nature of Prejudice* (Cambridge, Mass.: Addison-Wesley, 1954).

45. Triandis and Davis, *op. cit.*

46. F. Douglass, *Life and Times of Frederick Douglass: The Complete*

Autobiography (New York: Collier Books, 1962), 366-67 (original edition in 1892).

47. Rayford W. Logan, *The Negro in the United States: A Brief History* (Princeton, N.J.: Van Nostrand, 1957).

48. J. L. Jackson and A. F. Poussaint, "A Dialogue on Separatism," *Ebony* 25 (August 1970), 62-68.

49. Bennett, *op. cit.*, 37-38.

50. J. B. Rotter, "Internal versus External Control of Reinforcement," *Psychological Monographs* 80 (No. 609, 1966).

51. Coleman *et al.*, *op. cit.*

52. For extreme examples of this phenomenon in public schools in the Deep South, see M. Chessler, *In Their Own Words* (Atlanta: Southern Regional Council, 1967).

53. U.S. Commission on Civil Rights, *Racial Isolation in the Public Schools.* More recent evidence for this distinction is provided in: S. Koslin, B. Koslin, R. Pargament, and H. Waxman, "Classroom Racial Balance and Students' Interracial Attitudes," (unpublished paper, Riverside Research Institute, New York, 1970).

54. Another white observer enthusiastic about black separatism even denies that the conclusions of the contact studies are applicable to the classroom and other institutions which do not produce "continual and extensive equal-status contact under more or less enforced conditions of intimacy." Stember selectively cites the investigations of contact in public housing and the armed forces to support his point (C. H. Stember, "Evaluating Effects of the Integrated Classroom," *The Urban Review* 2 [June 1968], 30-31); but he has to omit the many studies from less intimate realms which reached the same conclusions—such as those conducted in schools (T. F. Pettigrew, "Race and Equal Educational Opportunity," *Harvard Educational Review* 38 [Winter 1968], 66-76) and employment situations (Harding and Hogrefe, *op. cit.*; Kephart, *op. cit.*; MacKenzie, *op. cit.*; and Williams, *op. cit.*), and even one involving brief contact between clerks and customers (Saenger and Gilbert, *op. cit.*).

55. Irwin Katz, *op. cit.*; and I. Katz, "The Socialization of Competence Motivation in Minority Group Children," in D. Levine (ed.), *Nebraska Symposium on Motivation, 1967* (Lincoln: University of Nebraska Press, 1967).

56. T. F. Pettigrew, "Social Evaluation Theory: Convergences and Applications," in D. Levine, *op. cit.*

57. Pettigrew, "Race and Equal Educational Opportunity."

58. U.S. Departments of Labor and Commerce, *The Social and Economic Status of Negroes in the United States, 1969* (Washington, D.C.: U.S. Government Printing Office, 1970), 5-7.

59. *Ibid.*

60. Bennett, *op. cit.*, 38.

61. A. Campbell and H. Schuman, "Racial Attitudes in Fifteen American Cities," in The National Advisory Commission on Civil Disorders, *Supplemental Studies* (Washington, D.C.: U.S. Government Printing Office, 1968), 5.

62. *Ibid.*, 19.

63. *Ibid.*, 6.

64. W. Brink and L. Harris, *The Negro Revolution in America* (New York: Simon and Schuster, 1964); and W. Brink and L. Harris, *Black and White: A Study of U.S. Racial Attitudes Today* (New York: Simon and Schuster, 1967).

65. P. Meyer, *A Survey of Attitudes of Detroit Negroes after the Riot of 1967* (Detroit, Michigan: Detroit Urban League, 1968); P. Meyer, *Miami Negroes: A Study in Depth,* (Miami, Florida: *The Miami Herald,* 1968); and Center for Urban Education, "Survey of the Residents of Bedford-Stuyvesant," unpublished paper, 1968.

66. *Ibid.*

67. H. E. Ransford, "Isolation, Powerlessness, and Violence: A Study of Attitudes and Participation in the Watts Riot," *American Journal of Sociology* 73 (March 1968), 581-91.

Part One
Assimilation and the Schools

1. Melting Pot: Myth or Reality?

Andrew T. Kopan

Since very early times people have been moving across the face of the earth, ever seeking more satisfactory situations. During the ancient period there were mass movements such as the barbarian invasions, but gradually they became what is now known as immigration. For hundreds of years there was little intellectual interest in the movements of people. With the nineteenth century came the realization that such movements were causing economic, social, religious, political and other problems, many of which have persisted down to our day, and, since the turn of the century, students have become concerned with the study of immigration and its effects not only upon the immigrant himself but also upon the nation. Problems affecting the immigrant often extended to his children and grandchildren. Descendants of European immigrants in the United States have largely become acculturated, but the nation is yet confronted with bringing into the mainstream of American life the newer "immigrants"—the migrant populations of Spanish-speaking Americans, American Indians, Appalachian whites, and Negroes.

Origins of the American People

Every nation has had its immigration and emigration problems. But the mass immigration that took place to the United States is unmatched elsewhere. In the more than 350 years since the English established their first permanent settlement at Jamestown, some 45 million people have migrated to these shores. This figure is many times greater than the American population in 1776. It is several times the number of people now living in the eight Rocky Mountain states. The peopling of America adds up to the greatest migration of all time, dwarfing all other population movements before or since.

Just a little more than a century ago Walt Whitman, the poet of democracy, hailed the United States as a "nation of nations." No phrase better sums up this country's cosmopolitan history. America was discovered by Scandinavians, named by a German mapmaker in honor of a Florentine explorer, and opened for colonization by a Genoese sea captain in the Spanish service. Captain Columbus' crew was a preview of things to come. It included an Englishman, a Negro, an Irishman, a Jew, and probably several Greeks.[1]

Non-Europeans got here long before Columbus. Will Rogers, the Oklahoma humorist who was part Cherokee, liked to say that his ancestors met the Mayflower when it was docked. Yet, like the Pilgrims, the first Indians were immigrants. In the distant past, according to anthropologists, the Indians migrated from Siberia across the Bering Strait and displaced the aboriginal American population. Where the earlier population originated has not been determined.

But the question of who came first is irrelevant. What is important is that, whether one traces his family back to Ellis Island, Plymouth Rock, the Bering Strait, or Africa, every American realizes that his ancestors came here from somewhere else. That is what President Franklin D. Roosevelt, who was of Dutch ancestry, meant when he reminded the Daughters of the American Revolution: "Remember, remember always, that all of us ... are descended from immigrants ... "

But Americans have not just come from somewhere; they have come from almost everywhere. Immigration explains why the people of this nation are unique in the diversity of their ancestry. They spring from a multitude of stocks that have made their way to this land from Europe, Asia, Africa, the Middle East, and Latin America.

This diversity has affected almost every aspect of United States history. Like the westward movement, to which it was related, immigration was a creative force in the shaping of American society. American culture emerged from the interplay between immigrant heritages and the New World environment. Our language; our government, politics, and economy; our religions, music, arts, literature, and sciences; our educational systems; our sports, entertainment, even much of the food we eat—all testify, in one way or another, to immigrant cultural backgrounds.

But immigration was, and remains, a two-way process. To know that immigrants altered America is not enough. We also have to see how America altered the immigrants. Otherwise, we fail to understand the meaning of the journey for the immigrant and for his children as well. The wilderness and the frontier changed the institutions the immigrants brought with them,[2] as did the melting pot theory and the concept of cultural pluralism.

The "Old" Immigration

Long before the American colonies were settled, Spanish and French explorers left their mark on the vast American wilderness. The Spanish influence is found in a wide arc across the southern part of the country, from Florida through Texas and New Mexico to California. The French influence is apparent up and down the Mississippi and Ohio River valleys.

The first wave of settlement came with the colonists at Jamestown in 1607 and at Plymouth in 1620. It was predominantly English in origin. The urge for greater economic opportunity together with the desire for religious freedom led these people to leave their homes. Of all the groups that have come to America, they had the most difficult physical environment to master, but the easiest social adjustment to make. They fought a rugged land, which was hard, but they built a society in their own image, never knowing the hostility of the old toward the new that would face succeeding groups. Although the original states were former English colonies, the inhabitants were by no means wholly English in origin, customs, or religion. The southern back country was settled by Germans, Scotch, Scotch-Irish, and Welsh. Along the southern seaboard, however, the English predominated. Similar backgrounds characterized the people of Pennsylvania. French Huguenots were conspicuous in Charleston, South Carolina; Swedish Lutherans in Delaware; Dutch Calvinists in New Amsterdam and Albany, New York; Roman Catholics in Maryland; and Greek Orthodox in Florida. By 1750 New York City was already on its way to becoming the most cosmopolitan city in the world. Forty years later, when the first U.S. census was taken, a little more than half the people in this country were of African, Scottish, Scotch-Irish, Welsh, German, Dutch, Swedish, Spanish, French, and other non-English stock, and they were divided into more than a hundred religious denominations.

Shortly after 1820, the first year in which the Census Bureau records foreign immigration, there was a considerable Irish influx. This movement reached its height in the late 1840's and the 1850's, owing chiefly to the severe potato famine and other causes of internal discontent and unrest in Ireland. About the same time the first considerable migration of Germans to this country began—a migration that was to continue in increasingly large numbers down to the early 1880's. The crushing of the liberals in Germany in 1848 (when Carl Schurz came to America and Karl Marx went to England), together with the economic difficulties at about the same time, were the motivating factors in this movement. During the same period, or a little later, many Swedes, Norwegians, and Danes also came to the United States, settling mostly in the upper Midwest.

The Rise of Nativism

Until 1885, by far the major number of foreign immigrants to the United States came from the countries of northwestern Europe. With few exceptions these settlers were of Teutonic and Celtic origin, possessing ideals, customs, standards of living, modes of thought, and religious beliefs similar to those of the earlier settlers: illiteracy was uncommon; education was highly esteemed; for the most part, homes were established in farming communities; and, except for the Germans, and, to some extent, the Irish, there was little tendency among the newcomers to settle in ethnic groups. Before 1880 immigration presented few obstacles to successful Americanization.

A major group that did meet obstacles, even though they were of Celtic origin, were the Irish Catholics. The advent of large numbers of these people in the eastern cities, and the establishment of their church schools, was looked upon by many Americans (themselves descended from earlier immigrant groups) as a menace to national security, and it resulted in a strong nativist movement. Protestant America's fear of Irish Catholics and of popery led to the burning of

schools and convents and to riots in cities such as Boston, Philadelphia, and New York. In New York City an extended controversy
over the use of public school funds by Irish Catholics resulted in the
establishment of the first real public schools there in 1852. A political party, the Know-Nothing party, was even organized in 1853 to
oppose Catholics and immigrants, especially Irish and Germans who
urged that the United States intervene politically in their homelands.
The party urged restriction of immigration, but the outbreak of the
Civil War diverted the attention of the country.[3]

The New Immigration

About 1885 America's immigration patterns changed. No longer
did the majority of immigrants come from northwestern Europe;
instead, larger and larger waves came from southern and eastern
Europe. Where before 1885 nine-tenths of the immigrants had come
from northwestern Europe, by 1905 three-fourths of them came
from countries in southern and eastern Europe. Their religion was
predominantly Roman Catholic, Greek Orthodox, or Jewish; customs, habits, and, to some extent, ideals formed striking contrasts to
those of northern and western Europe. Illiteracy ranged from 13.7
percent to 78.9 percent in Serbia. Moreover, the various Slavic
groups such as the Ruthenians, the Czechs, Croatians, Ukrainians,
and Poles were a "subject people" unfamiliar with the democratic
processes of western Europe and the United States. Furthermore,
this "new" immigration, including Italians, Greeks, and the Jews,
tended to settle in ethnic colonies in large cities, thus isolating themselves from the mainstream of American life. Most serious, perhaps,
was the fact that, unlike earlier immigrants, many of the latecomers
did not intend to make America a permanent home, and they had no
desire to become Americans.

The Beginning of Restriction

This "new" immigration, as it was called, began to alarm WASPish
America. Articles and books were written urging that the entry of
these "inferior" people into America be restricted. Organizations
such as the American Protective Association were formed to urge
Congress to pass legislation against the new immigrants. Several bills

were passed by Congress, but, with the exception of the Chinese Exclusion Act of 1882, they were vetoed by presidents Cleveland, Taft, and Wilson.

Finally in 1907 Congress appointed a commission to study all aspects of immigration and its effect upon the country. The Dillingham Commission, which set out to prove that the "new" immigrants were inferior to the "old" immigrants, made its report (in forty-two volumes) to Congress three years later.[4] Throughout the report were sprinkled reflections in scattered phrases and sentences about the inferiority of the new immigrants and their lesser capacity to be Americanized:

the Serbo-Croatians had "savage manners," the South Italians "have not attained distinguished success as farmers" and are given to brigandry and poverty; and although the "Poles verge toward the 'northern' race of Europe," being lighter in color than the Russians, they "are more high-strung," in this respect resembling the Hungarians. "All these peoples of eastern and southern Europe, including the Greeks and Italians . . . give character to the immigration of today, as contrasted with the northern Teutonic and Celtic stocks that characterized it up to the eighties. All are different in temperament and civilization from ourselves."[5]

This notion was based on the belief that the national origin of an immigrant was a reliable indication of his capacity for Americanization. It was said, and science seemed to show, that some people, because of their racial or national constitution, were more capable of becoming Americans than others. It was argued, further, that the "old" immigrants who came to the United States before 1880 were drawn from the "superior" stocks of northern and western Europe, while those who came after that date were drawn from the "inferior" breeds of southern and eastern Europe.

The "findings"[6] of the Dillingham Commission have long since been discredited, but not before they enabled Congress to pass legislation restricting immigration. Oscar Handlin, who has done much to discredit these findings, has stated that, while the differences between the "old" and the "new" immigration are significant, they have too often been exaggerated.[7]

An enormously popular book typical of the literature of this period was Madison Grant's *The Passing of the Great Race,* which was adjudged a "work of solid merit." Grant insisted that, unlike the older immigrants, the newer ones did not belong to the Nordic race.

The new immigration contained a large and increasing number of the weak, the broken, and the mentally crippled of all races drawn from the lowest stratum of the Mediterranean basin and the Balkans, together with hordes of the wretched, submerged populations of the Polish ghettos. "Our jails, insane asylums, and almshouses are filled with this human flotsam and the whole tone of American life, social, moral, and political, has been lowered and vulgarized by them."[8] Grant insisted that, unless laws were passed to restrict this immigration, the Anglo-Saxons of the United States would be inundated and eventually wiped out—the passing of a great race.

The breakout of World War I created hysteria as to the loyalties of the "new" immigrants. President Theodore Roosevelt criticized "hyphenated Americans" who took sides in the European war, but many ethnic groups supported their homeland against the traditional enemy—Poles against Russians, Balkan Slavs against Austro-Hungarians, Germans against English and French. The German-American Bund marched down the main streets of many cities. This led to a crash program of Americanization in schools, factories, and churches. The purpose of the program was to assert Nordic superiority by persuading the immigrant to abandon his old culture and become an American. This "instant Americanism," with its unfortunate aspect of coercion, created an atmosphere of suspicion and distrust that has never fully been erased.

After the war, these same feelings of fear and doubt persisted. Because the immigrant was frequently accused of being radical, there were attempts to suppress his newspapers and organizations, to brand his culture inferior and unassimilable, to ignore his aspirations, and to intimidate him. Those who supported Americanization too frequently assumed that American culture was something already complete, which the newcomer must adopt in its entirety. Such attitudes and activities promoted the restriction of immigration, but they did not advance the assimilation of the immigrants already in America.

The Americanization movement is reflected in certain educational practices today. Instruction in German was banished from some public schools. (Indeed, more money had been spent by some large school systems to teach American children German than to teach immigrant children English.) Numerous states outlawed the teaching of any foreign language, which was not ruled unconstitutional by a Supreme Court until the Nebraska case of 1923. Many states outlawed private and parochial schools, and it was not until the famed Oregon case that the Supreme Court declared such laws unconstitutional, holding that the "child is not the mere creation of the state—parents have the right to nurture and educate him."[9]

World War I completely destroyed the traditional concept of a free America. The revelation of "hyphenated Americanism," combined with questionable but much-publicized results of physical and mental tests made upon soldiers drawn from various immigrant groups, gave new impetus to those forces opposing the new immigration, forces that had been gaining strength since 1881. The wholesale exodus from stricken European countries at the close of the war removed the last shreds of effective resistance, and a quota law limiting the volume of immigrants by using selection on the basis of nationality was enacted in 1921. These restrictions discriminated against immigration from southern and eastern Europe (quotas were based on the census of 1890, when immigration from southeastern Europe was just beginning to gain momentum), and the restrictions were increased in 1924. The law with its "national origins" clause, effective in 1927, limited the quota to 150,000, and it favored immigration from Britain. Hence, restriction was cultural rather than economic; it sought to maintain the "Nordic" culture. This law remained in effect until 1965 when President Lyndon Johnson signed the reform immigration act, abolishing the "national origin" system and removing discriminatory restrictions against southern and eastern Europeans and others.

It must be remembered that migration, whether external or internal, has been the fundamental social process that created the United States. Voluntary migrations from Europe and forced migrations from Africa built this nation, and the internal migration from East to West unified it. After the First World War, when migration from Europe was sharply reduced by the quota system, the internal migration from farm to city and from South to North and West was the major factor in the industrial expansion of the United States.

All of these migrations were regarded as unwelcome and socially destructive by groups already settled and partially acculturated. Those of English or Anglo-Saxon origins looked down upon the Irish, the Germans, and the Scandinavians, who, in turn, looked down upon the Italians, the Slavs, the Greeks, and the Jews. Today, their descendants look down upon the Puerto Ricans, the Mexican-Americans, and the Negroes, who, as the most recent immigrants or migrants are often considered inferior and a threat to what is "American," whatever that means. Thus, a recurring nativism continues to afflict our nation, creating numerous social, political, and educational problems. And yet, all the migrations had one purpose—the uprooting of peoples in order that they and their children might have a better chance, truly a part of the American dream!

The Melting Pot Theory

The idea of the melting pot is as old as the Republic. "I could point out to you a family," wrote the naturalized New Yorker, Jean de Crèvecoeur, in 1782, "whose grandfather was an Englishman, whose wife was Dutch, whose son married a Frenchwoman, and whose present four sons have now four wives of different nations. *He* is an American, who leaving behind him all his ancient prejudices and manners, received new ones from the new mode of life he has embraced . . . Here individuals of all nations are melted into a new race of men . . . " It was an idea close to the heart of the American self-image. But as a century passed, and the number of individuals and nations involved grew, the confidence that they could be fused together waned, as did the conviction that it would be a good thing if they were to be. In 1882 the Chinese were excluded, and the first general immigration law was enacted, to be followed by a steady succession of new and more selective barriers. Then, in the National Origins Act of 1924, the nation formally adopted the policy of using immigration to reinforce, rather than further dilute, the racial stock of early America.

This latter process was well underway and gaining momentum when Israel Zangwill's play, *The Melting Pot,* was first performed in 1908. The play was an instant success. It ran for months on Broadway, and its title was seized upon as a concise evocation of a profoundly significant American fact. One of its characters, David Quixano, the Russian-Jewish immigrant, a "pogrom orphan" who escaped to New York City, exults in the glory of his new country:

America is God's Crucible, the great Melting Pot where all the races of Europe are melting and reforming! Here you stand, good folk, think I, when I see them at Ellis Island, here you stand in your fifty groups with your fifty languages and histories, and your fifty hatreds and rivalries, but you won't be long like that, brothers, for these are the fires of God. A fig for your feuds and vendettas! Germans and Frenchmen, Irishmen and Englishmen, Jews and Russians—into the Crucible with you all! God is making the American . . . The real American has not yet arrived. He is only in the Crucible, I tell you—he will be the fusion of all races, the coming superman.[10]

Yet, looking back, it is possible to speculate that the response to *The Melting Pot* was as much one of relief as of affirmation, more a matter of reassurance that what had already taken place would turn out all right than encouragement to carry on in the same direction. No country made up of a diversity of immigrant peoples has as yet successfully solved the problem of mass amalgamation.

Zangwill's hero throws himself into the amalgam process with the utmost energy. By curtainfall he has written his American symphony and won his Muscovite aristocrat, and almost all concerned have been reconciled to the homogeneous future, including a German concert-master and an Irish maid thrown in for comic relief. But the doctrine of the melting pot was not dominant among the ethnic groups of the nation in the 1900's, and in significant ways it became less so as time passed. Individuals, in considerable numbers to be sure, broke out of their mold, but the ethnic groups remained. The experience of Zangwill's hero and heroine was not general. The point about the melting pot is that it did not take place.

It was once believed that the system of public education with its almost universal use of English would produce a nation unilingual and unicultural at base. The successful operation of this principle was taken for granted, for the public schools did help to acculturate and Americanize untold thousands of immigrants. Revisionist writers now question such statements,[11] but it was World War I that clearly established that the nation was not of one culture and one language and that neither Jacksonian democracy, with its assertion of the similarity and equality of all, nor the later theory of the melting pot had worked effectively. While the public schools were teaching in English, private schools, particularly certain parochial groups, Protestant, Roman Catholic, and some Greek Orthodox, were carrying out instruction in various foreign tongues. Both industrial centers and rural regions contained communities culturally distinct from their American surroundings and conscious of their separate identity.

These communities, especially those of the so-called "new" immigration, added constantly to their ranks from streams of newly arrived immigrants and from the American people's failure to practice their national theory of equality. These immigrants congregated for mutual protection in ethnic colonies, especially in the large cities, because they were denied entry (like the blacks later) into the broader community. The ethnic colonies served as decompression chambers or mutual protective groups, where "wops," "hunkies," or "kikes" (as they were often branded), forced by social pressure back into their ghettos, could seek their place among their own kind. Of low economic status and without an intelligentsia (except in the case of the Jews), leaderless and with a tendency to lose successful members since the price of success was often the severing of group ties, these immigrant communities hung on in most American cities, ignored by many and condemned by others as un-American.

Ethnic Communities

Thus there is ambivalence in the American character: the proclamation of the equality of all people as exemplified in the Declaration of Independence and the Federal Constitution, on the one hand; and the practice of discrimination and the denial of equality, on the other hand. It is this ambivalence that contributed in part to the development of ethnic communities. Rebuffed socially and often economically, the immigrant groups developed certain characteristics. Mutual benefit societies have been formed to assist members at times of sickness or death and, incidentally, to serve as social gathering places. Food stores and restaurants purveying familiar food have served as gossip centers where news is shared and stereotypes of thought and action are reinforced and preserved. In most communities a church follows the first signs of prosperity, as soon as the group is able to support a minister or priest. To many an immigrant his religion is the only experience that he can carry unchanged from his old home to his new. Whether or not a school follows the establishment of the church depends largely upon the leadership, for the demand for education is far from universal among immigrants, who are often illiterate. The development of schools is most apt to be stimulated by religious authorities seeking either to preserve the religious affiliation of a group exposed to alien ways or to enable a particular church to survive. Such schools, whether supplementary or full-time, have been organized by evangelical Scandinavians, Polish

Catholics, German Lutherans, Greek Orthodox, and Orthodox Jews, to name some. In these schools, the ethnic language, history, and traditions are taught to second and third generations of immigrants, sometimes alongside English studies. When not supported by religious leaders, such schools are usually the work of organization officials who see in the younger generation the only way to maintain organizations that originally grew up to protect newcomers.

When a community is sufficiently large and literate, there are publications in the native tongue to spread news of the old country and of the community itself and to interpret the affairs of the nation at large. Professional men within the group perform necessary services. Traditional forms of entertainment develop. The community in many instances becomes so complete that its members practically never leave it (except to move from one such community to another). They do not think in other terms, hardly read American news, rarely meet other people or make contact with the outer community. Such isolation as this exists most conspicuously in more or less separate industrial communities, but it is almost as characteristic of blocks in the ghettos of large cities (for example, Jewtown, Little Italy, Greektown, Little Lithuania, Little Warsaw, and Chinatown, among others, in Chicago). Although it can hardly remain so complete for more than one generation in a city, a new generation does not see the end of the old isolation.

It is characteristic of these American communities that they should be always on the move, each new wave of immigration or migration forcing an old community out of its old home and into a new one. On Chicago's near West Side, within the shadow of the downtown skyscrapers, a prestigious Anglo-Saxon community of the 1860's and 1870's, now the site of the campus of the University of Illinois at Chicago Circle and the location of Chicago's famed Hull House, became a German and Irish settlement during the 1880's, deteriorating into a slum. By 1900, Italians, Jews, and Greeks had taken over the area, and after World War II it was occupied by Puerto Ricans, Mexicans, and Negroes. Even with such movements, however, essential cultural features persist without reference to geographic location. Immigrant groups are more self-conscious in their areas of second settlement than in their original unit. It is only when many leave the ghetto that they know they have been in it. If the area of second settlement has become completely developed as an ethnic community before they enter it, it may take a third or a fourth move to make them realize that they have been part of a separatist entity in the midst of a larger whole.

These separate communities consist of a solid, group-conscious nucleus surrounded by a fringe that is gradually being worn away by intermarriage, education, participation in activities such as sports, and economic change. They are torn by internal conflicts between the generations, for the first generation of native-born children, subjected to external influences, differs sharply in ways and attitudes from the parents. The internal factors holding the communities together are weakened whenever immigration is reduced, and the attitude of the broader community gains strength and becomes the perpetuating force.

Of course, the force of economic pressure is constantly at work, breaking down isolation, producing physical mobility, encouraging contacts among members of different groups, and rewarding those who achieve financial success with scant regard for the group from which they come. Sociologists tell us that, from among the people of the "new" immigration, the Jews, Greeks, Syrians, and Armenians were the first to reach middle-class status, and this was due chiefly to their mercantile background.[12] Yet even as these groups climbed the socioeconomic ladder and moved out of the ethnic community, they retained much of their ancestral ethnicity down to the third and fourth generation.

Cultural Pluralism

We may argue whether it is "nature" that returns to frustrate continually the imminent creation of a single American nationality. The fact is that, in every generation throughout the history of the American republic, the merging of the varying streams of population, differentiated from one another by origin, religion, and outlook, has seemed to lie just ahead—a generation yet to come, perhaps. This continual deferral of the final melting of the different ingredients (or at least of the different white ingredients) into a seamless national web such as is found in the major national states of Europe suggests that we must search for some systematic and general causes for this American pattern of subnationalities and subcultures. It is not the temporary upsetting inflow of new and unassimilated immigrants that creates a pattern of ethnic groups within the nation; rather it is some central tendency in the national ethos that structures people, whether those coming in afresh or the descendants of those who have been here for generations, into groups of different status and character.

Fifty years after mass immigration from Europe ended, the ethnic pattern is still strong in the United States. Four major factors appear to have contributed to the survival of ethnicity:

1. After every wave of immigration strong sentiments of "nativism" resulted in prejudice against immigrants, forcing them to close ranks for protection and to isolate themselves into ethnic colonies.[13]

2. Cultural conservatives in the ethnic communities exhorted their compatriots to remain loyal to their religion, language, customs, and traditions. These flames were generally fanned by the immigrant press, whose editors were usually culturally conservative, as well as by the organized church.

3. Politicians exploited immigrants for their vote, and ethnic political organizations were courted by both political parties.[14]

4. Third and fourth generation descendants of immigrants desired to seek out their ancestral roots and to perpetuate ethnic traditions —foods, songs, dances—which gave them identity. This is not unlike the current movement among Negroes in their search for identity and an acceptable self-concept.

The mosaic of subcultures that thus characterizes the United States has given rise to the concept of "cultural pluralism," a concept supported earlier by John Dewey. In an address before the National Education Association in 1916, he said,

No matter how loudly anyone proclaims his Americanism, if he assumes that any one racial strain, any one component culture . . . is to furnish a pattern to which all strains and cultures are to conform, he is a traitor to an American nationalism.

. . . I find that many who talk the loudest about the need of a supreme and unified Americanism of spirit really mean some special code or tradition to which they happen to be attached. They have some pet tradition which they would impose on all.[15]

But it remained for Horace Kallen to bring the concept of cultural pluralism into prominence. As early as 1924 he opposed the melting pot theory and advocated that immigrants should be encouraged to develop their institutions and ways of life, thus contributing to the richness of American life. Writing in opposition to the growing restrictionist movement of the early twentieth century, he wrote,

Today the descendants of the colonists appear to be reformulating a Declaration of Independence. Again as in 1776, Americans of British ancestry apprehend that certain possessions of theirs, which may be lumped under the word "Americanism," are in jeopardy. The danger comes, once more, from a force across the water, but the force is this time regarded not as superior, but as inferior. The relationships of 1776 are, consequently, reversed. To conserve the inalienable rights of the colonists in 1776, it was necessary to declare all men equal. In 1776 all men were as good as their betters; in 1920 men are permanently worse than their betters.[16]

Kallen reminds us that, when the English settlers arrived, they did not consider themselves different from the Englishmen of the mother country, for they possessed the same ethnic and cultural unity and were homogeneous with respect to ancestry and ideals. Not until the economic-political quarrel arose did they begin to regard themselves as other than Englishmen. They had forgotten how they had left England in search of religious liberty. They had forgotten how they had left Holland, where they had found this liberty, for fear of losing their ethnic and cultural identity, a condition which their descendants would deny to latecomers.

In 1924 Kallen's cry was a voice in the wilderness, overwhelmed by the voices of the restrictionists. Now, nearly fifty years later, cultural pluralism has become a reality.

How does it work? Basically today's affluent society has a "mass culture."[17] Since a culture is a common and standardized set of ways of thinking and believing, a mass culture is one in which most people think and believe alike. They share a maximum of goods and services. They have the same amusements. They generally read the same newspapers and view the same television programs. They eat approximately the same food and wear the same clothing. Goods are manufactured for a mass market. Popular taste and popular fashion are thus undifferentiated. The image of a mass culture is conveyed by the thought of millions of families watching Bob Hope. Some people sit in four-hundred-dollar chairs and divans in their penthouse apartments, while others sit on soiled, rancid, overstuffed sofas in ghetto slums, but all participate in the mass culture. Generally characteristic of mass culture is mass political behavior, led by astute politicians who tend to be manipulators. Mass behavior tends to be hypernationalistic, racist, or class conscious, depending upon the society. This is the secondary level of relationship in which most Americans participate.

On the primary level of relationship, which is the more intimate level that involves family, relatives, and friends, however, most Americans belong to subcultural groups, whether they be ethnic, religious, social, or economic. These are sometimes called "deviant cultural groups."

Some of the "deviant cultural groups" are made up of transitional social groups that are moving into the mass culture. In the United States these are the southern rural or Appalachian whites, southern rural Negroes, Puerto Ricans, Mexicans, and some eastern and southern Europeans. Several of these groups are classified as "culturally deprived," or "socially disadvantaged." They generally enter the mass culture by becoming acculturated to it. For instance, the family from the southern mountains that came to the North twenty years ago to work in the factory found great rewards by becoming acculturated to the mass culture of the North. Since then, the children have gone to school and have good jobs. The family has bought a small house in an industrial suburb. When they drive back in their automobile during a paid vacation to see their relatives, they return as heroes.

Alongside the mass culture are a number of other "deviant cultural groups." Some are religious groups; some are second- or third-generation ethnic groups; others are social-class groups. The sociological terminology speaks of "elites" and of "high culture," though these terms are not fully applicable to the contemporary situation. These deviant groups operate in some kind of tradition—literary, religious, ethnic, or aesthetic—and their productivity, use of time, and life style are determined by this tradition. The deviant groups judge the quality of their products (material, intellectual, or artistic) by standards that are independent of the consumer of the product. Their mores, music, colleges, eating habits, home furnishings, and favorite television shows reflect these standards and separate them from the mass culture.

The tendency in contemporary society is for the mass culture to grow at the expense of subgroup cultures. Transitional social groups tend to lose their identity (with the exception of blacks and other visible groups) and are swallowed up or assimilated by the expanding mass culture. As a result, cultural uniformity grows. While the poor people seek to join the mass culture and to work for acculturation or assimilation, those cultural groups that cherish their identities seek to escape the mass culture which they think threatens to engulf them. In both cases, education is the major instrument for achieving their goals. Education in contemporary American society is used to acculturate some groups to the reigning culture (the traditional role of public schools), as well as to acculturate other groups into deviant cultures which they think are better than the reigning culture (the traditional role of private schools and of some parochial schools). Education is a way of joining the American society for some people and a way of escaping the regimentation and standardization of American society for other people.

Hence, the melting pot, so gloriously expounded by Crèvecoeur two centuries ago and praised by Zangwill's characters some sixty years ago, is in reality a myth. The melting pot, as we have seen, simply failed to melt. And while it is a good general rule that, except where color is involved, the specifically *national* aspect of most ethnic groups rarely survives the third generation, and despite the intermarriages which continue apace so that even strong national traditions are steadily diluted, the groups do not disappear. The religious aspect serves, along with the other major factors mentioned, as the basis for a subcommunity, and a subculture continues to exist for these groups. Beliefs and practices are modified to some extent to conform to an American norm, but a distinctive set of values is nurtured in the social groupings defined by religious affiliation. This is quite contrary to early expectations. It appeared to Crèvecoeur, for example, that religion as well as national identity was being melted into one by the process of mixed neighborhoods and mixed marriages.

Religion and race, therefore, seem to define the major groups into which American society is evolving as the specifically national aspect of ethnicity declines.[18] Consequently, America remains a nation of mosaics—of cultural pluralities. For while most Americans, on the secondary level of relationship, participate to one extent or another in the mass culture, other Americans, on the primary level of relationship, participate in the culture of their subcommunity. The concept of cultural pluralism has resulted in a variegated and dynamic culture, each group contributing toward its enrichment. Herein lies the message for our schools. They should provide for this cultural diversity by offering their clientele alternatives to a standard curriculum.

Cultural pluralism has given America its strength. Immigration has made the United States a world power of over 200 million people. The immigrants that came to America, both white and black, tilled the fields, manned the industries, built the railroads, and did many other things that made the country the industrial giant that it is. As its motto—*E pluribus unum*—proclaims, the United States remains truly one nation out of many people.

Notes

1. Arthur Mann, *Immigrants in American Life* (Boston: Houghton Mifflin Co., 1968), 2; Seraphim G. Canoutas, *Hellenism in America* (New York: Cosmos Publishing Co., 1918), 20-21. I am indebted to Professor Mann for this section of the paper.

2. For a general account of the difficulties experienced by immigrants and the impact of the American social order upon them see Oscar Handlin, *The Uprooted* (New York: Grosset and Dunlap, 1951); Michael Kraus, *Immigration: The American Mosaic* (Princeton, New Jersey: D. Van Nostrand Co., 1966.)

3. A standard work on this topic is Ray A. Billington, *The Protestant Crusade, 1800-1860: A Study of the Origins of American Nativism* (New York: Macmillan Co., 1918).

4. For a synoptic view of the Dillingham Report, see U. S. Senate, 61st Congress, 3rd Session, Senate Document No. 747, *Abstracts of the Reports of the Immigration Commission, II* (Washington, D. C.: U. S. Government Printing Office, 1911).

5. As quoted in Oscar Handlin, *Race and Nationality in American Life* (New York: Doubleday Anchor Books, 1957), 85.

6. Despite the bias in the "findings" of the Dillingham Commission, which studied all aspects of immigration over a three-year period, its reports are nonetheless important for their statistical information, to wit: by 1911, in the public schools of the nation's thirty-seven largest cities, "*two out of every three* school children were the sons and daughters of immigrants." U. S. Immigration Commission, *Abstract of the Report of the Children of Immigrants in Schools* (Washington, D. C.: U. S. Government Printing Office, 1911), 18-19. For a review of the distorted findings of the Commission, see Handlin, *Race and Nationality*, ch. 5.

7. Handlin, *Race and Nationality*. See also Maldwyn Allen Jones, *American Immigration* (Chicago: University of Chicago Press, 1960), 3-5; ch. 8.

8. Madison Grant, *The Passing of the Great Race in America* (New York: Charles Scribner's Sons, 1916).

9. Clark Spurlock, *Education and the Supreme Court* (Urbana: University of Illinois Press, 1955), 162-68.

10. As quoted in Nathan Glazer and Daniel Patrick Moynihan, *Beyond the Melting Pot* (Cambridge, Massachusetts: M.I.T. and Harvard University Press, 1963), 289.

11. Colin Greer, "Public Schools: The Myth of the Melting Pot," *Saturday Review* 52 (November 15, 1969), 84-85; see also Colin Greer, *Cobweb Attitudes: Essays on Educational and Cultural Mythology* (New York: Teachers College Press, Columbia University, 1970), ch. 1; Charles E. Silberman, *Crisis in the Classroom* (New York: Vantage Books, 1970), 53-61.

12. Bernard C. Rosen, "Race, Ethnicity, and the Achievement Syndrome," *American Sociological Review* 24 (February 1959), 47-60.

13. A study of this newer nativism is to be found in John Higham, *Strangers in the Land: Patterns of American Nativism, 1860-1925* (New Brunswick, New Jersey: Rutgers University Press, 1955).

14. For example, until recently the position of postmaster general in Chicago always went to a person of German descent, certain high-ranking positions in the city to members of the Irish community, certain municipal judgeships to members of the Jewish, Italian, and Greek communities. The practice continues, as is illustrated by an item from the *Chicago Sun-Times* of August 26, 1970, under the heading "Jurist Slate—'A Melting Pot' " which includes this statement: "Democrats have put together another carefully balanced, 'something for everyone,' slate of candidates for associate circuit judge, including an Irish Catholic, a Pole, a Jew, a Greek, and two Blacks."

15. John Dewey, "Nationalizing Education," *Addresses and Proceedings of the National Education Association* 54 (1916), 184-85.

16. Horace M. Kallen, *Culture and Democracy in the United States* (New York: Boni and Liveright, 1924), 69.

17. I am indebted to Professor Robert J. Havighurst for certain sociological concepts used in this paper. See his "The Acculturation Process" in Ernest V. Anderson and Walter B. Kolesnik (eds.), *Education and Acculturation in Modern Urban Society* (Detroit: University of Detroit Press, 1965), 1-15.

18. Glazer and Moynihan, *op. cit.*, 314

2. Persisting Ideological Issues of Assimilation in America

Implications for Assessment Practices in Psychology and Education

Alfredo Castaneda

Assumptions underlying today's educational philosophies for the culturally different child in general, and the Mexican-American child in particular, can be traced to two basic ideologies concerning the nature of assimilation in America: the idea of a "melting pot" versus that of "cultural pluralism." Within the melting pot category, one must determine whether the result is exclusive or permissive. And, within the cultural pluralism category, one must determine whether pluralism is mandatory or optional in character.

Each of these factors will be briefly described from a historical perspective to assess their impact on conclusions drawn from sociological, anthropological, and psychological data derived from the study of Mexican-Americans. How they affected educational practice and philosophy will also be explained, and the cultural pluralists' position will be redefined in order to show the value of democratic cultural pluralism and biculturalism in education.

This paper was prepared for the Subcommittee on Compensatory Education, Work Group on Values, Social Science Research Council and funded by Project Follow Through, United States Office of Education. This chapter has been reprinted, with some revision, from *Education for 1984 and After*, published by the Study Commission on Undergraduate Education and the Education of Teachers, 1971. Reprinted by permission.

The Exclusivist Melting Pot: Anglo-Conformity

The Anglo-Conformist view of the melting pot has produced a variety of notions concerning racial superiority and exclusionist immigration policies, but its central assumption rests on the desirability of maintaining English institutions (as modified by the American Revolution), the English language, and English-oriented cultural patterns. This view of the melting pot is exclusive in that assimilation is considered desirable only if the Anglo-Saxon cultural pattern is adopted as the ideal.

This view of America as a crucible into which all non-Anglo-Saxon ethnic groups would melt received its fullest expression during the so-called "Americanization" movement that swept the United States during World War I and lasted into the 1920's and the 1930's. While the movement had more than one emphasis, it was essentially an attempt at "pressure-cooking" assimilation[1] that would strip the immigrant of his native culture and attachments and make him over into an American in the Anglo-Saxon image. The exclusionist tone and flavor of the movement can be vividly appreciated in the writings of one of the more noted educators of that day, E. P. Cubberly. This educator characterized the new southern and eastern European immigrants as "illiterate," "docile," lacking in "self-reliance" and "initiative," presenting problems of "proper housing and living, moral and sanitary conditions, honest and decent government and proper education." American life, Cubberly thought, had been made difficult by the presence of these new groups:

Everywhere these people settle in groups or settlements, and to set up their national manners, customs and observances. Our task is to break up these groups or settlements, to assimilate and amalgamate these people as a part of our American race, and to implant in their children, so far as can be done, the Anglo-Saxon conception of righteousness, law and order, and our popular government, and to awaken in them a reverence for our democratic institutions and for those things in our national life which we as a people hold to be of abiding worth.[2]

These remarks by Cubberly have been somewhat lengthily recorded because they are the ideological precursor for many of today's assumptions concerning the relatively low academic achievement of many Mexican-American children, and they have influenced current efforts at compensatory education. For example, Cubberly's remarks imply that the "manners," "customs," and "observances" existing in the child's home and community, that is, his culture, are inferior and need to be replaced, "in so far as can be done," to use Cubberly's own phrase, with the Anglo-Saxon cultural ideal.

Despite claims of "objectivity," these ideological strains continue to pervade the social sciences in one form or another. A current example is Celia Heller's book, *Mexican American Youth: Forgotten Youth at the Crossroads.*[3] The anthropological study completed by Kluckhohn and Strodtbeck in 1951[4] served as one of the important bases on which Heller arrived at a number of conclusions about Mexican-American youth. She supports the conclusion that "Mexican-Americans are the least Americanized of all ethnic groups in the United States and that this condition is largely the result of the child rearing practices of the Mexican-American family." If Mexican-Americans are to be "Americanized," according to Heller, their socialization practices must be changed. Heller also concludes that Mexican-American homes "fail to provide independence training," that the "indulgent attitudes" of Mexican-American parents tend to "hamper" their "need for achievement," and that strong kinship ties among Mexican-Americans create "stumbling blocks to future advancement by stressing values that hinder mobility."[5] According to Heller's statements, it is these socialization practices that hinder the Mexican-American child's ability to profit from school, for they are in direct contrast to Anglo-American middle-class culture and aspirations. The focus of attack, therefore, has been on the socialization practices of the Mexican-American home and community and the basis of attack stems from exclusivist Anglo-Conformist views of the melting pot.

The Permissive Melting Pot

The exclusive Anglo-Conformist version of the melting pot has probably been the most prevalent ideology of assimilation in America, but a competing viewpoint with somewhat more generous and idealistic overtones also has had its adherents and proponents since the eighteenth century. Conditions in the virgin continent modified the institutions which the English colonists brought with them from the mother country, and immigrants from non-English homelands such as Sweden, Germany, and France were exposed to this same environment. Thus, starting with the French-born writer, Crèvecoeur, in 1782, a new social theory of America as a melting pot came into being. Was it not possible, Crèvecoeur asked, to think of the evolving American society not simply as a slightly modified England but rather as a totally new blend, culturally and biologically, in which stocks and folkways of Europe were, figuratively speaking, indiscriminately (permissively) mixed in the political pot of the emerging nation and melted together by the fires of the American influence and interaction into a distinctly new type? This idealistic and ostensibly permissive notion of the melting pot became one of the forces for the open-door immigration policies of the first three-quarters of the eighteenth century, before the influx from eastern and southern Europe. But it omitted two indigenous peoples—the Native Americans and the Mexicans of the Southwest—from consideration, as well as that group forcibly brought to America, the Afro-Americans. In effect, the ideal type for the permissive view of the melting pot did not differ too greatly from the Anglo-Saxon ideal.

The vision projected was of some new and uniquely "American" cultural phenomenon. Embedded in this new vision, however, was the notion of supremacy whereby the result of the melting process was envisioned as being superior to any of the individual ingredients before melting. In this connection some remarks made in 1916 by the noted American educator-philosopher, John Dewey, are worthy of examination:

I wish our teaching of American history in the schools would take more account of the great waves of migration by which our land for over three centuries has been continuously built up, and made every pupil conscious of the rich breadth of our national make-up. When every pupil recognizes all the factors which have gone into our being, he will continue to prize and reverence that coming from his own past, but he will think of it as honored in being simply one factor in forming a whole, nobler and finer than itself.[6]

Thus, Dewey's vision of the superiority of the melted product over the individual ingredients seems easily inferable from his statement, "nobler and finer than itself," which clearly seems to say that one's own cultural heritage is all right but, when it has melted with others, the result will be even better. Despite liberal overtones, this permissive interpretation of the melting pot carries a hidden message of

cultural superiority: the uniquely American cultural form which results will be better, if not the best. The message for the child who has
not yet "melted" is clearly negative: what he is is not enough; there
is something "nobler and finer."

Cultural Pluralism

A central issue in cultural pluralism concerns the right of the
minority ethnic group to preserve its cultural heritage without at the
same time interfering with "the carrying out of standard responsibilities to general American civic life."[7] Paradoxically, the hope for an
"integrated" nation held by both the exclusive and permissive adherents of the melting pot theory served to produce ethnic enclave
through the dynamics of prejudice and institutionally sanctioned discrimination.

In an attempt to establish communal societies in order to preserve
a corporate identity, ethnic groups solicited Congress as early as
1818 formally to assign national groups to a particular land base.[8]
Spurred by the melting pot vision of an integrated national society,
however, Congress denied these petitions and established the principle that the United States government could not be used to establish
territorial ethnic enclaves. Thus, while de jure ethnic communalities
could not be, the social forces of prejudice and discrimination laid
the basis for the evolution of present-day de facto communalities
that maintain their unique cultural styles in communication, human
relations, and teaching or child socialization practices. "Cultural pluralism" has been a historical fact in American society, and it continues to the present.

Basically, theories of cultural pluralism fall into two categories:
those which hold that pluralism is mandatory, often associated with
separatist or nationalist notions; and those which hold that pluralism
is optional.

Mandatory Cultural Pluralism

In a two-part essay printed in the *Nation* in 1915, Horace Kallen,
one of the earliest of the ethnic cultural pluralists argued that "the
United States are in the process of becoming a federal state not
merely as a union of geographical and administrative unities, but also

as a cooperation of cultural diversities, as a federation or common-wealth of national cultures."[9] Kallen proposed this to be the more or less inevitable consequence of democratic ideals since individuals are involved in groups and democracy for the individual must, by impli-cation, also mean democracy for the group. Thus, Kallen interpreted the term "equal" as it appeared in the Declaration of Independence, the Preamble, and amendments to the Constitution to support the concept of "difference," and asserted that the term "equal" is an affirmation of the right to be different. It was in this connection that the term *cultural pluralism* was coined. While Kallen's writings have many aspects, his theme of a "federation of nationalities" with the implication that the individual's fate is predetermined by his ethnic group membership caused some distress within the ranks of other cultural pluralists.

Optional Pluralism

Kallen's emphasis on the theme that the individual should retain his ethnic identity caused considerable discomfort, particularly for two other educators who basically subscribed to the theory of cul-tural pluralism. These two educators, Berkson[10] and Drachsler,[11] adopted the position that different ethnic groups should have the right to maintain an ethnic identity and even proposed a variety of ways this might be done, including ethnic communal centers and after-public-school-hour ethnic schools. Both men favored efforts by the ethnic community to maintain communal and cultural life, pro-viding a rich and flavorful environment for successive generations, and they suggested that the government should institute a program emphasizing knowledge and appreciation of the various cultures in the public schools. This idea of legitimization of numerous ethnic communities and their cultures was labeled "cultural democracy" by Drachsler, and he felt that it should be added to older ideas of political and economic democracy. These ideas of democracy, he maintained, implied freedom of choice. Here is where the earlier cultural pluralists introduced the irrelevant dilemma of choice applied to education, particularly at the time the child enters school. These two educators put the issue this way: while cultural pluralism may be democratic for groups, how democratic is it for individuals, since the choice of whether to melt or assimilate should be a free one?

That this question of choice is still with us today can be seen in the work of Milton Gordon from whose book, *Assimilation in American Life,* published in 1964, I have drawn liberally. Gordon's own remarks in his concluding chapter should be fully quoted in order to clearly identify this dilemma of choice:

> The system of cultural pluralism has frequently been described as "cultural democracy" since it posits the right of ethnic groups in a democratic society to maintain their communal identity and subcultural values . . . however, we must also point out that democratic values prescribe free choice not only for groups, but also for individuals. That is, the individual, as he matures and reaches the age where rational decision is feasible, should be allowed to choose freely whether to remain within the boundaries of communality or branch out . . . change . . . move away, etc. Realistically, it is probably impossible to have a socialization process for the child growing up in a particular ethnic group that does not involve some implicitly restrictive values . . .[12]

Gordon's statement, "that it is probably impossible to have a socialization process for a child growing up in a particular ethnic group that does not involve some implicitly restrictive values," resembles the notions often applied to Mexican-Americans: they are "clannish," "stick to their own kind," "refuse to become American," and others. Furthermore, it reflects a lack of awareness of the newly evolving notion of biculturality.[13] Quite in contrast to Gordon's observations, the more typical picture in the American public school is that it confronts the Mexican-American child with choice at a stage in his life when such "mature and rational decisions" are not possible. Finally, Gordon's statements ignore other possibilities, namely that, if the mainstream environment abides by the ideal of democratic cultural pluralism, it will be enriched by different cultural forms and loyalties. The educational institution continues, even today, to maintain policies of exclusion, omission, and prohibition that deny the Mexican-American child his culturally democratic right to explore freely the mainstream cultural environment using those cultural forms and loyalties he has learned at home and in his community.

The version of cultural pluralism that is to be examined in the following section is more properly called democratic cultural pluralism. Its goal, as far as education is concerned, is biculturalism.

Biculturalism: The Educational Goal of
Democratic Cultural Pluralism

Table 2-1 reviews the set of assumptions underlying the goal of biculturalism in education. The left column denotes a characteristic of the community, for example, the degree to which traditional Mexican values predominate (traditional), whether both Anglo-American and Mexican-American values are more or less equally present (transitional), or whether Anglo-American values predominate (urban).

These clusters of values in a given Mexican-American community are considered to be determinants of the socialization or child-rearing practices of the home and community, as can be noted in the next portion of Table 2-1 labeled "Socialization practices of home and community." It is assumed that the cultural values predominating in the community strongly influence child socialization practices in four distinct areas: (1) communication style, for example, whether English, standard Spanish, or Barrio Spanish is spoken, or any combination of these; (2) human relation styles, for example, the importance of the extended family, the degree of personalism, and so forth; (3) incentive-motivation style, that is, those methods which the child learns as appropriate for obtaining support, acceptance, and recognition in his home and community; and (4) the methods or styles of teaching that the child experiences from his mother, father, siblings, the extended family, and others.

Each of these four general categories or factors are further assumed to determine four important characteristics of the child described under the general heading, "Learning style of the child." It is these four important, firmly developed, general characteristics with which the child enters school: (1) a preferred mode of communicating, for example, speaking Spanish only, some or Barrio Spanish, nonstandard English; (2) a preferred mode of relating to others such as expecting personalized direction from adults; (3) a preference for certain incentives over others, for example, he might be more inclined to be motivated by rewards emphasizing achievement for the family over achievement for the self or group versus individual goals; and, finally, (4) a cluster of cognitive characteristics which reflect his preferred mode of thinking, perceiving, remembering, and problem solving.

Table 2-1. Assumptions underlying biculturalism in education

Variations in cultural values	Socialization practices of home and community	Learning style of child	Areas of change for creating a culturally democratic educational environment
1. Traditional	1. Communication style	1. Preferred mode of communication	1. Communication
2. Transitional	2. Human relation	2. Preferred mode of relating	2. Human relation
3. Urban	3. Incentive-motivation style for obtaining support, acceptance and recognition	3. Incentive preference	3. Incentive-motivation
	4. Teaching style	4. Preferred mode of thinking, perceiving, remembering, and problem solving	4. Teaching and curriculum

The conflict many Mexican-American children experience centers in one or more of these four areas because most educational institutions are characterized by educational styles—preferred modes of communicating, relating, motivating, and teaching—characteristic of the Anglo-American middle-class culture. These styles are considered, by virtue of one form or another of the melting pot ideology, to be the ideal modes which all children must acquire. If the child possesses different modes, he is then viewed as "culturally deficient," "culturally impoverished," "passive," "lacking in achievement motivation," "having a language handicap," or, more brutally, "mentally retarded." If the educational policy of the school excludes, ignores, or prohibits expression of modes different from the ideal, we characterize it as a culturally undemocratic educational environment for any child whose modes of relating, communicating, motivation, and learning are different from the preferred educational style of the school.

The last section of the table, then, delineates areas for change in the school environment: (1) communication, (2) human relations, (3) incentive-motivation, and (4) teaching and curriculum. In order to provide a culturally democratic educational environment for the Mexican-American child, such changes must facilitate, incorporate, and adapt to the learning style of the child as outlined in the third column of the table.

With this type of analysis, it is possible to specify those areas of institutional change that the school must consider if it is to provide a culturally democratic educational environment ensuring equal educational opportunity for any child. This version of the concept of cultural democracy, as far as the school is concerned, simply means the right of each child to experience an educational environment that accepts his preferred modes of relating, communicating, motivation, and learning as equally important. The goal of education becomes biculturalism, which simply means that the child is allowed to explore the mainstream culture freely by using those preferred modes he brings to school from his home and community. Thus, this notion of cultural democracy, or democratic cultural pluralism, in education clearly requires a bicultural educational environment in any school confronted with the responsibility of providing equal educational opportunities for children whose home and community differ culturally from the mainstream.

Some Historical Antecedents

One of the earliest pieces written in the United States by a psychologist was concerned with instructing teachers about the "cognitive styles" of children. It was entitled, "The Contents of Children's Minds," by G. Stanley Hall.[14] Contrary to the popular beliefs of the time, Hall believed that the thinking of children differed from that of adults; it was not simply a miniature cognitive version, and the best way for the teacher to acquire information about the unique or cognitively different modes in children was to study (assess) the child himself. Hall's study, reported in "The Contents of Children's Minds," dealt with children in the Boston public schools in the early 1880's. He developed a questionnaire method (now considered to be the forerunner of many of today's psychological tests) that could be easily used by teachers. His basic assumption in conducting the study was that curricular planning and development in teaching methods must be based on the recognition that the thought content and process of the child differed from that of the adult. Hall did not assume, and presumably the Boston public school educators did not assume, that such differences implied that children were "disadvantaged" in any particular way. The content and processes of a child's thought simply differed from that of an adult. On the basis of information acquired through Hall's questionnaire method, the Boston public schools created an educational environment compatible with the child's cognitive characteristics; he was accepted as he was and it was the school's obligation to modify its educational style and process accordingly.

Unfortunately subsequent developments in the decades following Hall's pioneering work led the educational testing movement in the United States along different lines. Rapid developments in statistical methods, the impact of work done by Galton, Cattell, Thurstone, Pearson, Binet, and Wechsler, and increasing pressure on the schools for evaluation—all served to contribute to a comprehensive education testing program in the public schools that focused on the measurement of intelligence, ability, and achievement, permitted the development of quantitatively based descriptions of children ("gifted," "slow learner," "underachiever," "educable mental retardate"), and served as the foundation for such educational practices as tracking, ability grouping, and special classes for "educable" or "trainable" mentally retarded children. More recently varieties of these tests of ability, intelligence, and achievement have been used for purposes of identifying, selecting, and evaluating many aspects of compensatory educational programs for the minority poor, such as Head Start and Project Follow Through.[15]

The rather technical and somewhat esoteric aspects of these tests, as well as the fact that many were standardized essentially on children of the middle class, have had two major consequences. First, a barrier was created between the individual teacher and the intent, meaning, and potential value of the tests due, essentially, to the evolution of a sophisticated technical superstructure describable in a new and special language and set of concepts and increasing restrictions imposed on their use by such newly evolving professional groups as psychometrists and educational psychologists. Second, the preponderance of testing, focusing as it did on ability, achievement, and intelligence with instruments that reflected the linguistic and communication styles, the human relation and teaching styles of the middle-class community precluded the teacher from getting similar information for children of the poor and culturally different. The testing movement has proved culturally undemocratic. Tests developed and standardized on the minority poor and culturally different, which reflect their communication, human relation, and learning styles, have not been part of the fabric.

Recent Developments in Cultural Influences on Learning and Incentive-Motivation Styles

A culturally democratic educational environment is, by implication, knowledgeably prepared to teach the culturally different child—or any child, for that matter—in his (a) preferred mode of communicating, (b) preferred mode of relating, and (c) preferred mode of obtaining support, acceptance, and recognition, and (d) his preferred mode of thinking, perceiving, remembering, and problem solving. Unless school assessment programs provide the teacher of the culturally different child with pertinent information in these areas, her professional function as a teacher will be compromised. Assessment programs, guided by the psychologist, can be devised to provide the teacher with information and concepts that link these four areas to the educational process of the school. For the present, however, we shall restrict our review to incentive-motivational and cognitive styles.

In a rather comprehensive study by Stodolsky and Lesser,[16] first-grade children representing membership in four different ethnic groups—Chinese, Jewish, Negro, and Puerto Rican—were tested with a variety of "intellectual ability" measures to determine the presence of differential patterns of ability among the four groups. The results showed, for example, that, in the case of Jewish children, their pattern of abilities reflected greater strength in verbal ability and weakness in spatial conceptualization. Chinese children, on the other hand, exhibited a pattern just the reverse of that of the Jewish children; they were relatively strong in spatial conceptualization and weaker in the verbal dimension. These differential patterns were found to remain essentially the same for the children within the same cultural group regardless of whether they were of a low-class or middle-class socioeconomic background.

One interpretation of these findings stresses that these differential patterns relate to differences associated with preferred modes of learning stressed within a given cultural group. Different cultural groups differ in their teaching styles in that they produce differences in the preferred modes of perceiving, remembering, thinking, and problem solving (preferred modes of learning); one cultural group (Jewish) stresses the verbal dimension, and the other (Chinese) stresses the spatial dimension.

Is this important information for the teacher to know? It is inordinately better than an I.Q. or achievement score in that it has more direct implication for teaching strategies or teaching styles. Thus, in teaching Chinese children, it may be advantageous to stress spatial dimension as a framework for devising curriculum plans, thereby using a preferred vehicle of learning for Chinese children. This is the underlying principle in the Montessori method, at least that aspect which utilizes the tactile dimension as a vehicle for learning. The difference, however, is that the Montessori method makes the priori assumption that this is the preferred mode of learning for all young children. Our point is that it is necessary to determine for what groups of children this is the preferred mode of learning.

At this juncture it is critical to point out that the issue is not which should be the preferred mode of learning. From the administrative point of view one mode of learning may be preferred because it simplifies the administrative-managerial problems of the school. Where this view is the guiding policy, it disenfranchises those children with preferred modes of learning that differ from the school's preferred mode of teaching.

If we now focus our attention on evidence for culturally determined incentive-motivational preferences, more specifically along the dimension of relating cooperatively versus competitively, a study by Kagan and Madsen[17] represents a case in point. Competitive and cooperative behavior was studied in three groups of children of three different cultural groups, that is, Anglo-American, Mexican-American, and Mexican children. They found that performance on a simple task depended on whether reward was obtainable through cooperation or competition. When reward could be achieved only through cooperative behavior, performance on the task was best among Mexican children, with Mexican-American children coming next and Anglo-American children achieving the lowest scores. However, with the same task employed when rewards could be obtained only through competitive behavior, these positions were completely reversed. Anglo-American children performed best, Mexican-American children were next, and Mexican children had the lowest performance scores.

Kagan and Madsen's study offers some specific suggestions for viewing different cultural groups to determine differences in incentive-motivational systems for obtaining recognition, support, or acceptance from the environment. Is this important information for the teacher to know? Our answer is, yes, in view of the fact that it helps to delineate and specify for the teacher some of the important dimensions that should be considered in attempts to analyze critical dimensions for different groups of children which comprise the "student-teacher" relationship. Such information can provide suggestions for creating incentive and reward conditions that are culturally appropriate for different groups of children. On the basis of Kagan and Madsen's study, for example, Anglo-American children would be more effectively motivated by conditions that stress competitively obtainable incentives. On the other hand, Mexican-American and Mexican children would be more effectively motivated by conditions that stress cooperatively obtained incentives.

Notes

1. M. M. Gordon, *Assimilation in American Life: The Role of Race, Religion and National Origins* (New York: Oxford University Press, 1964).

2. Elwood P. Cubberly, *Changing Conceptions of Education* (Boston: Houghton Mifflin Co., 1909), 15-16.

3. Celia Heller, *Mexican-American Youth: Forgotten Youth at the Crossroads* (New York: Random House, 1966).

4. Florence Kluckhohn and Fred Strodtbeck, *Variations in Value Orientations* (New York: Row Peterson and Company, 1961).

5. Heller, *op. cit.*, 35.

6. John Dewey, "Nationalizing Education," *Addresses and Proceedings of the National Education Association* 54 (1916), 185-86.

7. Gordon, *op. cit.*

8. Isaac B. Berkson, *Theories of Americanization: A Critical Study with Special Reference to the Jewish Group* (New York: Teachers College, Columbia University, 1920).

9. Horace M. Kallen, "Democracy versus the Melting Pot," *Nation* (February 18, 25, 1915). Reprinted in Horace M. Kallen, *Culture and Democracy in the United States* (New York: Boni and Liveright, 1924).

10. Berkson, *op. cit.*

11. Julian Drachsler, *Democracy and Assimilation: The Blending of Immigrant Heritages in America* (New York: Macmillan Co., 1920).

12. Gordon, *op. cit.*, 262-63.

13. Stephen S. Baratz and Joan C. Baratz, "Early Childhood Intervention: The Social Science Basis of Racism," *Harvard Educational Review* 40 (Winter 1970), 29-50.

14. G. Stanley Hall, "The Contents of Children's Minds," *Princeton Review* 11 (1883), 249-72.

15. Eleanor E. Maccoby and M. Zellner, *Experiments in Primary Education: Aspects of Project Follow Through* (New York: Harcourt Brace Jovanovich, 1970).

16. Susan S. Stodolsky and G. Lesser, "Learning Patterns in the Disadvantaged," *Harvard Educational Review* 37 (Fall 1967), 546-93.

17. S. Kagan and M. C. Madsen, "Cooperation and Competition of Mexican, Mexican-American and Anglo-American Children of Two Years Under Four Instructional Sets," *Developmental Psychology* (in press).

3. The Americanization and Education of Japanese-Americans
A Psychodramatic and Dramaturgical Perspective

Reed Ueda

The Japanese and their culture have traditionally placed strong emphasis on persona or "face," on superficial impression, thus creating an elaborate system of demonstrative obligations and etiquette in which honor or the saving of face is of paramount importance as a device for social control and survival. A few examples of the liturgy of persona and appearance illuminate this facet of Japanese life. Japanese families and organizations have invoked *Hito ni wawareru* (others will laugh at you) and *Sonna koto wo shitara haji wo kaku* (such acts will bring disgrace) as guidelines for self-presentation and self-disclosure. As one scholar has put it, "The Japanese system appears much more norm oriented—the how, the style, and the means of interaction are important . . ."[1] Naturally, Japanese-Americans, as Japanese, have inherited this impressionistic value system and its set of operational mechanisms. Furthermore, their sensitivity to the projection of image—the persona they effect—has been acutely heightened by their status as a racial minority and the intense persecution to which they were subjected.

The thesis propounded in Erving Goffman's *The Presentation of Self in Everyday Life*[2]—that human beings interact like "performers" before an "audience" to convey carefully predetermined impressions of themselves—is especially germane to the analysis of the highly self-conscious and prepossessing experience of Japanese-Americans.[3] My primary assumption is that Japanese-Americans view experience in terms of dramaturgical interaction and that they dichotomize society into actors and audience. When they identify themselves as actors, they visualize themselves engaging in performances that are under the constant scrutiny of an audience with high expectations, which will socially endorse or invalidate the performance.[4]

Because of this dramaturgical concentration, which is continuous in Japanese history, Japanese-Americans have exploited the "arts of impression management"[5] in cultural contacts with whites; they have been consummate performers as quiet, nonthreatening, bland individuals,[6] and their very success at the dramaturgy of race relations has cut them off from their actual selves. They are so image-bound that the expression of natural, spontaneous feelings is strait-jacketed, and, like E. Franklin Frazier's *Black Bourgeoisie*,[7] they dwell in a world of unreality filled with illusions that seduce and convince the Japanese-American that he has "made it." The ironic fact is that the Japanese has "made it" only inasmuch as he has been able to fabricate an artificial and ingeniously contrived definition of self that conforms with philistine values in American society and that conceals the social turmoil and psychic suffering of the life he has led in this country.

The Japanese-American, as a consequence, is a fugitive human being, separated from his natural sources of feeling and spirit by the fear of losing face and destroying his defense system of images. It is important to keep in mind continuously that the arts of impression management were cultivated in large part as protection against a hostile white America. Although the Japanese were traditionally skilled in these arts by their culture, they were compelled to resort to them even more when they were faced with a persecutory environment.

While Goffman's brilliant but erratic book attempted to deal with personal relations in terms of the analytical concepts of performer, act, stage, and audience, I would like to transcend the microsociological level and employ his framework to examine race relations between Japanese and white Americans.

Moreover, whereas Goffman uses the concept of the "dramaturgical" to structure his mode of analysis, I would like to add a dimension to this operational definition by expanding it to include the psychodramatic since I believe that psychodynamic forces such as shame, guilt, and anxiety, which were generated jointly by the fear of white hostility and a traditional, repressive culture, have exerted inordinate influences upon Japanese-Americans in their social contacts.[8] Japanese social institutions and concepts have been generally dramaturgical, whereas the Japanese-American presentation of self has been specifically psychodramatic. In his studies on public schooling in Hawaii and California, Allison Davis characterized Japanese-Americans as "complex, stringent, and anxiety-ridden."[9] The following study, therefore, will be conducted on the lines of a psychodramatic analysis of the Japanese community and of the evolution of its relationship to white American society.

I will start with the individual. Even before his arrival, the Japanese immigrant was highly self-conscious because of his ponderously norm-oriented[10] culture, which rested on a code of honor, shame, and superficial etiquette. His self-consciousness grew as a result of the humiliating harrassment and abuse he faced as a foreigner. He adapted to the new situation, by adjusting his definition of self. He became an actor—the performer of the noncommital act. Such an act did not involve controversy, argument, or radically deviant behavior, for such a performance would damage prospects for survival in American society. Instead, conversation was avoided; an apologetic demeanor was cultivated; and hazardous social situations were mitigated by obsequious, embarrassed humor. To a substantial degree, the Japanese of today share this social methodology. They are reluctant to engage in potentially unseemly behavior, and they are not outspoken or strongly expressive because such adventuresome social forays carry a double risk: disruptions could occur that would ruin the presentation of the innocuous image to whites; also, if they staged a bad performance—stuttering, becoming nervous, committing faux pas—they would be painfully embarrassed and humiliated.

Overarching this complicated and nervous psychodramatic situation has been the historic *Enryo* syndrome. Enryo is an almost untranslatable term. It constitutes a vital part of the structure of Japanese social etiquette, and it originated out of the obsequious and deferential manner in which inferior individuals or groups related to their social superiors. Usage of this behavioral norm increased with the passage of time to encompass a multiplicity of interactional situations that included the proper way to behave around American whites, how to behave pleasantly in ambiguous social conditions, and how to disguise feelings of anxiety, embarrassment, and confusion.[11]

In short, the Japanese-American was constantly aware of his identity as actor, of the roles that he had to play in appropriate settings, and he was conversant with hypocritical routines required to mollify ambivalent social situations. These inhibiting psychodramatic circumstances have resulted in little deviant behavior,[12] creative or criminal, among Japanese, and, as a consequence, the cultural quality of Japanese-American life has lacked richness and diversity. The robust, aesthetic, and vigorous culture and personalities of the Japanese that Ruth Benedict and George Sansom admired perished in the welter of Japanese-white race relations.[13] Japanese-Americans have produced few charismatic leaders, cultural innovators, or individuals of high public profile. Their personalities have been vitiated by the diffidence and reserve that stem from their psychodramatic self-consciousness. These conditions have produced a singular lack of skill or passion for verbal argument, debate, banter, or humor, especially in contacts with whites. Most ethnic groups have invented folkloric ethnic jokes and stories (Jewish jokes, Polack stories, for example), whereas Japanese-Americans have created hardly any verbal counterparts. These facts are descriptive of the status of Japanese-Americans as half-human beings—fractionalized men incapable of functioning in the full range of dimensions that comprise human interactions.

I oppose such theories of Japanese assimilation because they fail to investigate the psychological agony and the negative personality effects of the psychodramatic presentation of self and also because they verge on being mythical immigrant success stories. These theories have stressed the congruence of Japanese cultural values with American customs and folkways, have equated Japanese American goals of socioeconomic self-improvement with American materialistic pursuit, and have overstressed the Japanese family as a nursery of discipline and industry that effectively equipped youths to compete in the market, schools, professions, and trades. Most speciously of all, they conclude that the Japanese have been smoothly absorbed into American society, with a few exceptions such as the evacuation, and have now found legitimate and abiding happiness in the United States.[14] I do not mean to imply that there are not truths to these theories; I merely seek to produce a more salutary balance in our understanding of the Japanese-American experience by offering the psychodramatic insight they have omitted.

The fallacy of these arguments is that they picture the Japanese as foreigners who were really incipient white Americans. These theories negate the differences that have existed between the Japanese and the Anglo-American civilizations; they downplay the degree and substantive nature of racial conflict; they belittle cultural pluralism, favoring, instead, ultimate absorption into an anonymous melting pot; they fail to appreciate the excruciating psychodramatic contortions and hypocritical liturgies the Japanese had to perform in order to effect the "right" definition of self that made them marginally tolerable to the American public.

A spurious corollary to these theories of Japanese race relations is the claim that the Japanese are a model minority. They have been exploited as proof of what Herbert Croly called "The Promise of American Life" and used as shills to verify that other minorities could "make it" given the discipline and diligence of the Japanese.

This [the Japanese American experience] is, of course, no isolated story, which concerns only one small ethnic group. It has much broader significance, particularly at this time when the gravest problems our nation faces revolve around the denial of full equality and justice to large segments of our population. It should give faith to all Americans in the validity of the ideal and the possibility that we can achieve it more fully.[15]

When we look back on the past prejudice faced by the Japanese, we find that even their most optimistic dreams have been surpassed. Such a story may give us optimism for the future of race relations in the American society.[16]

The stereotype of the successful Japanese-American is not only the result of good acting and stage technique on the part of the actor; it also requires an enthusiastic response from the white audience. That the defensive methods of impression management need a reciprocating counterpart in the form of the audience's tactful tendency to applaud and act protectively to "help the performers save their show"[17] cannot be overemphasized.

The audience applause of the American public has been instrumental in forging the ethnic star status of the Japanese-American actor upon the social stage. Hence, it is not too venturesome to assert that the stereotype of the successful Japanese-American is shrouded in the same aura of unreality that surrounds glamorous Hollywood celebrities, an aura manufactured to gratify the mythological expectations and cravings of America. The artist of impression management—the Japanese social actor—and the interested audience—the American public—have combined to make the Japanese-American the ethnic superstar, which satisfies the popular need to believe in the mythology of America as the land of opportunity and equality.

In turning to the Japanese as a community, Goffman's typology might well describe them as a "team of performers."

Though initially exposed to persecution because of their foreign looks, customs, and economic competition, the Japanese have steadily achieved structural assimilation because of well-calculated psychodramatic performances and image making. Because the Japanese are anxiously aware of their image, they have striven vigorously as a team of performers, from the first generation of Issei, to project a definition of self that would not provoke the white man but would eventually win his toleration or favor by establishing the persona of a hard-working, decent, uncomplaining, and obedient subordinate. These Issei teams usually assumed the form of a restaurant staff, a farming community, or a menial domestic service organization.

The Japanese community can still be accurately understood as an effective "performance team," a set of individuals who cooperate in staging a single routine.[18] Since they perceive that their prosperity in American society is contingent upon their ability to project the right image, the Japanese go about performing this act in grim earnest. The routine of defining a defensive, inconspicuous, nonthreatening self requires a high degree of social organization in a team of actors. Goffman has described this requisite situation with a threefold scheme that I have paraphrased and condensed:

1. *Dramaturgical loyalty.* In order to maintain the performance of a team, the team members are required to act as though they have accepted specified moral obligations to each other.

2. *Dramaturgical discipline.* The exercise of great self-control and discipline is mandatory for the preservation of the dramaturgical line being presented. Each team member must possess these essential qualities in playing out his role unwaveringly.

3. *Dramaturgical circumspection.* Discipline and loyalty are important, but are still not sufficient. It is necessary that the team and its constituent members use prudent foresight and careful planning in determining in advance the most effective way to present the performance.[19]

The Japanese community as a team of actors has been efficient in meeting these criteria for successful performances and has achieved astonishing group solidarity.[20] Japanese-Americans have been rigidly authoritarian and enjoined unwavering nondeviant behavior of all team members. In Japanese community papers, regular reports have appeared naming youths who have been arrested, specifying their crimes, their parents, and their home addresses in order to shame them and their parents and thus dispense punishment for departure from the routine of the performance. The Japanese community has also been honeycombed with channels of gossip. Unconventional behavior has been suppressed by the informal spreading of knowledge about dishonorable behavior to teammates who then scorn and ostracize the reprobate for his impropriety. Allison Davis reports that gossip in Japanese neighborhoods can be so powerful and cruel as to force families to move out. The Japanese family emphasizes strict loyalty and thoroughly trains children to abstain from outspoken behavior and to avoid controversial, potentially embarrassing, situations. Strict self-control and discipline are mandatory. The Japanese community-as-team has been a tightly knit group exercising endogamous marriage practices to maintain extreme cohesiveness by creating family ties. Sawtelle, one of the largest Japanese neighborhoods in Los Angeles, is substantially comprised of a handful of large family groups like the Mochizuki's and the Sakaniwa's to which many are related by marriage or blood. Resembling well-disciplined teams of actors, Japanese communities have ably practiced "dramatic circumspection," carefully pondering and planning the impressions that various group performances would make. The Japanese are very anxious about their future, which is not surprising when one considers the total abrogation of their civil rights during World War II, and they have established many organizations to prudently direct performances that convey the impression of civic-minded, patriotic activity. Organizations such as the Japanese American Citizen's League, all-Japanese boy scout troops, all-Japanese athletic leagues, and youth clubs attached to Buddhist, Baptist, and Methodist churches, each espousing the most rudimentary American values—all have worked to determine how effectively and in what form the Japanese community can stage its show.

The Japanese-Americans have created exceptional dramaturgical performances through such means. Harry Kitano describes the extraordinary display of the American virtues of cleanliness, neatness, and orderliness visible at annual Japanese community picnics:

At a signal, at the end of the day, all, even the tiniest children, set about picking up every last scrap of litter—every wrapper, every plastic spoon, every paper plate and cigarette butt, every tiniest fragment of potato chip. They leave the park as clean as they found it—cleaner than they found it. In fact, it will not be so clean and tidy again for another year.[21]

The presence of dramaturgical loyalty, discipline, and circumspection, as well as the team-like character of the group are obvious. There can be little doubt that such a performance could only leave a favorable impression upon the public audience.

Perhaps the most vivid symbol of the psychodramatic practices of Japanese-Americans is observable in their homes and in the appearance of their neighborhoods. Japanese communities are comprised of rows of neat, orderly looking homes. They are usually modest to the point of being nondescript, but they possess an aura of being well kept and antiseptically clean that is obvious even to the casual observer. It is as if the entire physical community were a stage upon which the image of American orderliness and neatness could be presented. Other symbolically middle-class paraphernalia appear inside the homes. Allison Davis remarked of Japanese-American homes in Hawaii that, "The furniture, decorations, and books in homes are overwhelmingly American. Teachers say that the middle-class Japanese-American home has more books than the white home of the parallel class."[22] The extreme concern for and care taken of the appearance of homes is one of the most concrete manifestations of the Japanese addiction to norms, external symbols, and the psychodramatic presentation of self in everyday life.

Pernicious consequences do flow from such a life. Maintaining a high level of consciousness of one's self as performer and one's self as self can be emotionally exhausting, induce paranoid tendencies, and create general anxiety. (Allison Davis, in his study of Japanese students and their families, observed that they were nervous and tension ridden.[23]) More fundamentally, the Japanese person as a social actor engaging in a psychodramatic presentation risks losing touch with his internal nature. This is because acting involves self-distantiation (playing at something one is not), which is a short step from self-alienation.

The good social actor is able to control and even to suppress inappropriate emotional reactions to personal problems, to mistakes and miscues on the part of his teammates, and to the appreciation or hostility expressed by his audience. He can stop himself from crying over what is tragic and from laughing about what is humorous. In short, the good social actor modulates, disguises, and represses spontaneous feelings in order to sustain the impression of the line presented, the "status quo," of his team's performance.[24] It is lamentable that, the more capable an individual becomes as a social actor, the farther he is from believing in the show he creates for others. He can experience a unique and ghastly kind of alienation of self and come to entertain an exaggerated wariness of others.[25]

The Japanese-American in attempting to present his American self has been cast adrift from aspects of his Japanese and, more important, of his human identity. This process is insidiously pathological for, as the act is repeated, the individual becomes less aware that he is only an actor. By repeated performance he arrives at a state where he cannot separate act from fact, and he loses consciousness of his self-alienation much as Marx's *lumpenproletariat* were unconscious of their own alienation.

Perhaps the most important point of this study is that psychodramatic behavior and consciousness were instrumental in reassimilating the Japanese into American society after their internment during the Second World War. Because the Japanese held that superficial symbols such as honor and face carried such power, they sought to recover white trust and structural reassimilation by presenting themselves as extraordinarily *American* Americans, by projecting an unimpeachable and vindicating persona of Americanhood. From a people who had been summarily imprisoned and whose confiscated property was recompensated at ten cents to the dollar, there came no sizable protest or complaint. Instead, they quietly aspired toward postwar bourgeois and patriotic goals, thereby attempting to prove that any suspicion of ideological or national disloyalty was groundless. By wholeheartedly engaging in postwar capitalistic opportunism for reassimilation purposes, the Japanese assayed to demonstrate that they had always accepted the American creed of democracy and equal opportunity and that they would demonstrate this fact and the validity of the creed in their very effort to "make it."[26] Further, they sought sweet revenge against white America by using persona control—putting on a good front to embarrass the American government and people into admitting that they had been wrong to evacuate the Japanese.

But this tactic was self-defeating in two ways. First of all, white Americans do not share the psychodramatic value system of the Japanese; they are not beleaguered by persona, honor, or shame to the same degree, and they are not as hypersensitive to exposures that cause embarrassment. The Japanese, in the postwar period, sought to embarrass the whites into repentance by model behavior, a tactic which would probably have worked on Japanese peers, but a tactic to which white America was largely impervious. White American tradition has never been as extremely sensitive to normative liturgies or norms invested with political and social power as the Japanese tradition has been. Thus, a majority of the American public still feels that the mass incarceration of the Japanese was justified; and even such an enlightened liberal as former Chief Justice Earl Warren still obdurately refuses to apologize for his leading role, as Attorney General, in agitating for evacuation.

Second, the intensive bourgeoisification of the Japanese in the postwar era, which was intended to display their loyalty, made it impossible for this potential sector of American society to engage in constructive social criticism or dissent. Certainly a half-century of persecution and evacuation provided ample grounds to establish a strong camp of Japanese dissenters or progressives. Or they could have pursued militant protest and aggressive political action along with civil rights activists and progressive political groups. Japanese-Americans have demonstrated a singular lack of imagination or sensitivity when they are faced with the issues of American politics. Instead, they unquestioningly wedded their futures to orthodoxy and consensus, and they stand today as pillars of the status quo. Presently more and more Japanese-Americans are registering in the Republican party.

Indexes of Japanese structural assimilation and the bypassing of other racial minorities can be seen in the results of a Survey of California State Civil Service Employees taken in 1963 and reported in a Japanese-American newspaper. It showed that for Asian employees (mainly Japanese) the modal income was $7,400 per year, almost $3,000 more than any other minority group employed in the civil service.[27] Statistics from the California census of 1960 revealed that the Japanese ranked first among all racial minorities in education and income.

These enormous strides reflected advantages in schools and training, so education in this period was especially significant for the Japanese. In fact, their involvement with educational self-improvement became a near-mania.[28] Education as a channel of upward mobility presented a pleasantly safe, but respectable definition of self. The Japanese have exhibited high achievement in school, and they are consummate actors before the teacher and the class. I propose again the viability of a psychodramatic interpretation as an explanatory model for Japanese-American success—this time specifically in the public schools. Japanese students, like good actors, are constantly on guard against disturbance of the performance. In order to avoid mistakes in presentation or offending people, they are reserved, self-conscious, and reticent to engage in disputatious, outspoken acts and utterances. In the "backstage," the Japanese family at home, the children are rigorously taught to respect authority and to obey their elders; on the "frontstage" of the classroom they are impeccable performers. They are anxiously deferential to the teacher and enthusiastically obedient to directions and orders. "My informants pointed out," remarked Allison Davis, "that when the average little Japanese-American child leaves home each morning for school his mother tells him be kind to the teacher."[29] It follows logically enough, then, that they are usually regarded by teachers as being among the best pupils in the class.

Japanese-language schools, established to transmit to the Nisei and the Sansei the core culture as well as the language of the home country, psychodramatically conditioned their egos and rendered them especially adaptable and amenable to the working of the American public school. In Hawaii and on the West Coast, most Nisei attended Japanese schools daily for one to two hours before or after attending the public schools. Discipline, work, obedience, and teacher authoritarianism were harsh and exacting, so much so that many Nisei informants have said to me that the public schools were "nicer places" than the Japanese schools. Indeed, strict and diligent habits of classroom behavior and performance were inculcated so that Japanese children were well trained in their language schools for proper performance roles in the public school system. The Japanese school defined the acting role and consciousness of the Japanese pupil so that he was culturally advantaged or, from another perspective, culturally susceptible to the educational techniques, homilies, and personality molding of the public school. He knew obedient behavior was expected of him, knew that he must study hard, and, above all, he knew his place in respect to the teacher and the power structure of the educational establishment. The Japanese-language schools enabled him to master the methods and roles of performance and acting that would lead to exceptional achievement.

But in this examination of the Japanese-American educational experience we must take the audience more fully into consideration. Japanese students are encouraged to play the role of "good student" because of the praise, as well as the pressure, they receive from proud parents and expectant teachers. Allison Davis noted that, in both California and Hawaii, white teachers loudly expressed the view that the best students were Japanese-Americans.[30] These teachers were fond of them and expressed this feeling in interpersonal contact, by entrusting Japanese pupils with "important" duties such as serving as monitors and by declaring to their parents that their sons and daughters were the finest children in class. As previously mentioned, for a successful performance to occur, the actor (the Japanese student) must get tactful applause from his audience (the school establishment), which is what historically happened.

Further, if one regards the class as a kind of "acting school" the teacher served as the dramatic model whom the students sought to emulate. The Japanese family had emphasized the imitation of model actors—father, mother, older brother or sister—at home and had also encouraged the child to follow the teacher as a model actor. Extending this metaphor, one can say that the teacher invented and directed dramaturgical routines to mold the students to "act" in her style. In Hawaii, where Japanese pupils composed 35 to 40 percent of public school enrollment, a teacher described a classroom dramaturgical liturgy intoned with ritualistic rhythm:

Instruction in civil government, hygiene, arithmetic, geography and sewing is good Americanism; the inculcation of patriotism through song, picture, poem, and dance is good Americanism. . . . Thus it is for each teacher of Hawaii to grasp every opportunity offered by the Course of Study and to exert influence to make the children of Hawaii good future citizens of the United States.[31]

This utterance is the litany of the model actor—the high priestess of the classroom who by exemplary conduct and enforced imitation of rites will inculcate the pupil with her routine style of performance and self-presentation in everyday life. The educational liturgy of dramaturgy imposed upon a people whose social institutions were dramaturgical and whose self-presentation was psychodramatic potently co-opted the personality of Japanese pupils.

> The Nisei was shaped in thought and action far more thoroughly than others realized by the American system. . . .
> By the time he entered high school, the boy had developed a fierce love for the United States, its history and traditions and all it stood for.[32]

The Japanese-American acquired the additional part of the well-educated man in his role of superstar ethnic actor. The character he portrayed was endowed with public schooling, and this appealed to the audience sufficiently to gratify the public's belief in the great school myth of educational opportunity and self-improvement.

The Japanese psychodramatic consciousness, habits, and view of the world made them eminently susceptible to American educational liturgy and dramaturgy, which was, therefore, a major causal factor for their high attainment in schools and their eventual structural assimilation. There may well be an organic relationship between the psychodramatic mode of group and interpersonal interaction, the educational success of the Japanese, and their structural assimilation, and this must be investigated in a detailed and thorough manner. My own hypothesis is that their exceptional achievement in education is genetically linked to the psychodramatic framework of their behavior. The nature of this connection demands exploration because it could help resolve the historical and contemporary problems of socialization and educational achievement. Scholars may find, by using the example of the Japanese-Americans, that the psychodramatic behavior structure is strongly conducive to high educational achievement, especially the educational improvement of immigrant groups, which probably is the same as saying that the psychodramatic behavior structure coupled with a large, effective educational plant is a powerful vehicle for co-optation in American society.

In this paper I have argued that the unique way in which the Japanese adapted to American society was to adopt a psychodramatic strategy toward whites, which was made more effective by their home country knowledge of rituals and techniques connected with impressionistic self-presentation. The inconspicuous, nondescript image they projected was dictated by the oppression and hostility they encountered in this country. In continuing to convey this image of themselves by what Goffman calls the "art of impression management"—the social controls of the Japanese community, and its team-like nature—the Japanese created a stereotype of themselves as discretely innocuous, pleasantly bland aliens who, with the inevitable abatement of initial white hostility, would be invited to assimilate into the socioeconomic structure provided that they kept themselves at a reasonably safe distance. In striving to produce these conditions for acceptance into American society, Japanese men and women have reduced themselves to the status of incomplete human beings. They are reluctant to express spontaneous feelings, display anger or passion in front of whites, take charge of groups, or engage in demonstrations of formal or informal protest and dissent. They cannot participate richly and deeply in the various modes of normal human behavior.

Through the fastidious psychodramatic presentation of a noncontroversial self, the Japanese male attained a nonsexual identity, and the Japanese female was made into an "ultrafeminine doll."[33] Japanese houseboys were favored in California because they projected a neuter, safe, and obedient image, whereas a black houseboy would not be preferable because he would be much more threatening in terms of his sexual identity and reputation for recalcitrance. The white businessman in his office would feel more comfortable knowing that the wife and daughters he left at home that morning were being attended by a Japanese houseboy instead of a black male. In terms of his sexual identity and image, it is fair to say that the Japanese-American man has been at least partially emasculated.

Of course to compare the Japanese-American male to the black American male involves an extreme juxtaposition. Even in comparison with white males, however, the Japanese male does not exhibit the average sexual normative identity. Arkoff, Fenz and Arkoff noted in a study conducted in Hawaii that Sansei third-generation males expressed a high need for deference, abasement, nurturance, affiliation, and order and that, in comparison to white males, they manifested a lower need for dominance, aggression, autonomy, exhibition, and heterosexuality.[34]

On the other hand, Japanese-American females were stereotyped as the epitome of pure femininity. Japanese women were preferred by white males because they were not castraters; they were docile, domestically efficient, and subordinate to the will of the husband. Allison Davis commented:

Most Japanese girls or women . . . still are characterized by their respect for authority in the family or school, their extreme decorum, their apparent docility, . . . their almost universal neatness, and unfailing courtesy. . . . Its greatest importance is that this pattern of neatness, decorum, and "docility" makes the Japanese-American girl seem the most ideal type of "wife" to many white males.[35]

Naturally one might expect to discover evidence of high or increasing incidence of mental illness among Japanese-Americans owing to the degree of repression, rigidity, and self-control that dominates their social lives. Official statistics show, however, that there is no excessive amount of mental illness among Japanese Americans. But these statistics are secondhand formal notations and do not indicate the realities of psychic afflictions in the Japanese community. Out of their great fear of disgrace, Japanese families maintain a high tolerance, usually based on suppression, for members who display *kichigai* or insane behavior. Furthermore, the ethnic community serves as an umbrella under which release from certain tensions can occur without being registered in official records or noticed by the public. Because of these two factors of potential disgrace and ethnocentrism, Japanese are not likely to seek professional assistance outside of the community.[36]

It is reasonable to ponder how much neurotic and psychotic behavior goes untreated and unreported. Two important facts are highly suggestive of an underground psychic pathology that has been concealed by the psychodramatic behavior pattern. First, schizophrenia is the most common form of mental illness among Japanese and may be strongly related to the self-alienating process of the psychodramatic presentation of self. Second, there is an outstanding rate of somatization—exaggerated concern with bodily functions and the acquisition of psychosomatic and nervous disorders—among Japanese-Americans.[37] The repressive forces and pressures of Japanese social life may find release in the form of weird internal maladies.

Ironically enough, crime, which is often linked to mental disorders, may be a manifestation of salubrious Japanese personality development. Japanese-American communities and police departments are aware that crime statistics among Sansei have climbed rapidly and deplore this fact. It is my opinion that this index of social deviancy is an important sign that the younger generation has acquired a new capacity for expressiveness, assertiveness, and adventurous rebelliousness that has rounded them out as more completely developed human beings. It is not my point to condone criminal behavior, but one should not view rising rates of crime among younger Japanese as a wholly negative phenomenon often confused with moral corruption and mental disturbance. It may be a positive manifestation of the efforts of the younger Japanese to win their humanity.

The addiction of Japanese to psychodramatic interaction, the belief that events, persons, and things are controlled and defined by exterior qualities, has not only produced difficult personality consequences and problems. It has created serious, large-scale political and social problems.

First, the desire to present the innocuous persona made the Japanese abysmally apolitical; they have been afraid to take controversial stands because this would tarnish their image as loyal Americans. Secondly, the proper presentation of self has made them concerned with subjects that relate exclusively to enhancing the proper presentation of self. Thus the Japanese are rushing into the pit of pragmatic amorality. They have realized that securing bourgeois goals has pragmatic value for the purposes of the right presentation of self, and thus they support capitalism in a mindless, headlong, and amoral fashion.

This state of affairs brings us to a dialectical impasse. Goffman has noted that insofar as individuals are performers they will be profoundly concerned with sustaining an image or impression that will fulfill the standards and expectations by which the audience judges them. The sheer number, pervasiveness, and ubiquitousness of these standards impose a moral order upon the world of performers, but, as performers, individuals do not concern themselves with the moral goal of fulfilling standards. Instead they focus on the amoral objective of fabricating a convincing impression that these standards are being realized and the moral order is being followed. Social actors in one sense, then, can be said to operate in a milieu of moral issues, but, as performers, they have little or no concern with them.[38]

Thus the Japanese-American's view of the school has lacked true moral content. The school is seen merely as a training center for the skills that will lead to a position in the middle-class structure of

American society. This, in my opinion, explains, in large part, the dearth of artists, rebellious intellectuals, and creative cultural non-conformists among educated Japanese-Americans.

Third, the Japanese social actor's preoccupation with presenting a definition of self acceptable to the white American public has cut him off from potential alliances with blacks, Chicanos, Puerto Ricans, native Americans, and other disadvantaged groups. Affiliation with these groups who have not projected as "good" an image of self as the Japanese would wreck the routine of the Tomming performance of the Japanese-American community-as-team. This is because a good staging effect is dependent upon a carefully composed cast of actors chosen for their appropriateness to the performance. Certainly militant blacks would be inappropriate cast members for the play staged by the Japanese.

On the West Coast, a Third World movement of Chicanos, blacks, Asians, and native Americans is coalescing in the form of community-based organizations that seek to provide political education and cooperative self-improvement.[39] It is a hopeful sign that Japanese psychodramatics will become obsolete through generational change and that they will be able to unite with other minorities in effective cooperation directed toward securing equal socioeconomic opportunities and rewards and the elimination of institutional and psychological racism. The first step, as St. Augustine and Karl Marx have said, is to gain consciousness—consciousness of the untruths in which one lives. The Japanese-American must become conscious of the ambient psychopathology of dramaturgy and image making and transcend it. Then we can hope that the true faces of the Japanese-Americans will emerge from behind the masks and their voices, expressive of their trying experiences as a minority in America but so long stifled by the caution of psychodramatics and racist oppression, will finally become audible.

As E. Franklin Frazier pointed out about the black bourgeoisie,[40] Japanese-Americans must realize that their deep involvement in the psychodramatic presentation of self has induced a milieu of unreality and bogus image creation.

The Japanese community-as-team rehearses and presents over and over again the image by which they desire to be represented. The myth of the Japanese as a racial minority that achieved success is paraded in Japanese newspapers, periodicals, and community organi-

zations. The most trivial events involving Japanese-Americans are reported in these media in order to make the importance of the successful Japanese more vivid. In the late 1960's, the *Rafu Shimpo,* a
Japanese daily in Los Angeles, published a preposterous front-page
article about a Japanese person whose news value consisted of the
fact that he had gotten into a minor traffic accident with Sam Yorty,
the mayor of Los Angeles. The Japanese are now heavily engaged in
an egotistical presentation of self *to themselves.* Whether or not this
alluring veil of pseudoreality and narcissism can be torn away will be
a crucial question for the future of Japanese-Americans. But this
much is clear: the Japanese-American must convert himself from
social actor to genuine individual vis-à-vis white Americans; he must
disabuse himself of the flattery of ethnic superstar; and he must rid
himself of the worshipful reverence of American schools that blinds
him to the co-optive power it has exerted over him. Lastly, he must
stop regarding the American public as an audience to please, and he
must dismantle the theater of the Japanese-American community
upon which he has so long hung his mask.

Notes

1. Harry H. L. Kitano, *Japanese Americans: The Evolution of a Subculture*
(Englewood Cliffs, New Jersey: Prentice-Hall, 1969), 113.
2. Erving Goffman, *The Presentation of Self in Everyday Life* (Garden City,
New York: Doubleday Anchor, 1959), 1-16.
3. Kitano, *op, cit.,* 94-115.
4. Alicia O. Matsunaga, lecture on contemporary Japanese culture, February
1966, University of California, Los Angeles.
5. Goffman, *op. cit.,* 208-36.
6. Bill Hosokawa in his *Nisei* (New York, Morrow, 1969) indicates this char-
acterological trait in his subtitle *The Quiet Americans.*
7. Frazier posits that, in spite of the alluring make-believe world which serves
the middle-class blacks as a refuge, they are nevertheless plagued by frustration,
anxiety, insecurity, and guilt. See E. Franklin Frazier, *Black Bourgeoisie* (Glencoe, Illinois: Free Press, 1957).
8. Hosokawa, *op. cit.,* 171-89; Allison Davis, "The Public School in America's Most Successful Racial Democracy: Hawaii," unpublished report, Chicago,
1947, 30-35.
9. Davis, *op. cit.,* 32.
10. "Norms," as defined by Kitano and as used in this study, are shared
meanings, social signs and symbols, in a culture that help to establish the background for communication and interaction. Hence the social norm's chief func-

tion is to provide a guide for correct social behavior so that an individual has an acceptable method of conducting interpersonal relations and, conversely, is capable of assessing the acts of others and passing judgment upon them.

11. Kitano, *op. cit.*, 103-105.

12. *Ibid.*, 116, 133.

13. Ruth Benedict, *The Chrysanthemum and the Sword* (Boston: Houghton Mifflin, 1946); George Sansom, *Japan, A Short Cultural History* (New York: Appleton-Century-Crofts, 1943).

14. Kitano, *op. cit*; Hosokawa, *op. cit.*

15. Edwin O. Reischauer, "Foreword," in Hosokawa, *op. cit.*, xii.

16. Kitano, *op. cit.*, 229.

17. Goffman, *op. cit.*, 229.

18. *Ibid.*, 79.

19. *Ibid.*, 212-28.

20. Shotaro G. Miyamoto, "Social Solidarity among the Japanese in Seattle," *University of Washington Publications in the Social Sciences*, II (December 1939), 57-130. This is a sociological examination of the Japanese community in Seattle, depicting its powerful and impressive internal solidarity before the Second World War. It relates family, economic, religious, educational, and political institutions to group solidarity.

21. Kitano, *op. cit.*, 93.

22. Davis, *op. cit.*, 35.

23. *Ibid.*, 30.

24. Goffman, *op. cit.*, 217.

25. *Ibid.*, 236.

26. Toshio Yatsusshiro, Iwa Ishino, and Yoshiharu Matsumoto, "The Japanese-American Looks at Resettlement," *Public Opinion Quarterly* 8 (Summer 1944), 188-201. These authors, who were evacuated from the West Coast to Poston Relocating Center, argue that resettlement is a challenging invitation to freedom for the evacuees and an equal challenge to the American government and public that could prove that freedom and opportunity truly distinguished this nation.

27. *Nichi-bei Times*, December 3, 1963 (English section).

28. Reed Ueda, "Historical Issues of Education in Hawaii," unpublished paper, Chicago, 1972, 10-11.

29. Davis, *op. cit.*, 32.

30. *Ibid.*

31. Ruth C. Shaw, "Americanization and the Course of Study," *Hawaii Educational Review* 8 (December 1919), 26.

32. Bill Hosokawa, "Prologue," in Hosokawa, *op. cit.*, xvi.

33. Eldridge Cleaver, *Soul on Ice* (New York: McGraw-Hill, 1968), 176-90.

34. Abe Arkoff, "Need Patterns in Two Generations of Japanese-Americans in Hawaii," *Journal of Social Psychology* 50 (1959), 75-79.

35. Davis, *op. cit.*, 32.

36. Kitano, *op. cit.*, 124-28.

37. *Ibid.*, 126.

38. Goffman, *op. cit.*, 251.

39. In Los Angeles, for example, there is an organization known as "The Storefront" that coordinates and sets up educational activities, cultural events, and mutual aid in the black, Chicano, and Asian communities.

40. Frazier, *op. cit.*, 174-94; 213-32.

Part Two
Black Experience:
Segregation to Community Control

4. Making the Schools a Vehicle for Cultural Pluralism

Barbara A. Sizemore

Today the schools are in trouble. The youth are in rebellion. High schools are so chaotic in some places that they must close to reorganize. They reflect the society and the times since education is a product of that society and culture and is the deliberate or purposeful creation, evocation, or transmission of knowledge, abilities, skills, and values.

Silberman cites mindlessness as the cause of what is wrong with the public schools. He defines mindlessness as the failure or refusal to think seriously about educational purpose, the reluctance to question established practice. This analysis completely avoids the discussion of purposeful action, thereby eliminating forceful cultural imperatives such as racism. Consequently, Silberman falls victim to a classic educational error: the inaccurate definition of the problem.[1] Such inaccurate definitions lead to the wrong solutions. This paper will attempt to discuss (1) the meaning of culture, pluralism, and related concepts; (2) the values emanating from the culture; (3) the educational system produced by this value system; and (4) a model for change.

If the schools reflect the society and the culture, then certain

From *Cultural Pluralism in Education: A Mandate for Change,* edited by Madelon D. Stent, William R. Hazard, and Harry N. Rivlin. Copyright 1973 by Fordham University. Reprinted by permission of Appleton-Century-Crofts, Educational Division, Meredith Corporation.

cultural imperatives may operate as causes. In man's attempt to preserve and reproduce himself, he has been in constant conflict with
the land, nature, and other men. Sekou Toure defines culture as the
"expression in particular and specific forms of a general problem—
that of the relationships linking man to his environment."[2] These
relationships are greatly affected by differentiations in the structure
of the object world with regard to orientation to the polarity of
gratification and deprivation.[3]

Egos interact with social objects called alters and with nonsocial
objects. Social objects have expectations which are oriented toward
egos producing a complementarity of expectations. This system can
be analyzed in terms of the degree of conformity of ego's action with
alter's expectations and vice versa, and the contingent reactions of
alter to ego's action are sometimes called sanctions.

The effect of these sanctions is determined by ego's need-disposi-
tions and the ability of alter to gratify or deprive. There, then, is a
double contingency inherent in such interaction. Ego's gratifications
are dependent on his selection among available alternatives and alter's reaction will be determined by ego's selection. This double contingency produces the precondition for cultural patterns. Thus complementarity of expectations in the processes of human interaction is
central in the analysis of the cultural patterns.

In this social order where so many groups with varying cultural
patterns reside, pluralism and desires for inclusion confound the
double contingency and the complementarity of expectations. Pluralism is the condition of cultural parity among ethnic groups in a
common society. Cruse says that "America is an unfinished nation—
the product of a badly-bungled process of inter-group cultural fusion . . . [and] it has effectively dissuaded, crippled and smothered
the cultivation of a democratic cultural pluralism in America."[4] Most
excluded ethnic groups strive for inclusion or full participation in the
social order with preservation of ethnic differences.[5] The obstacles
to the attainment of inclusion are the institutions which perpetuate,
promote, and preserve the symbolic systems of the dominant ethnic
group (alter).

The great myth that the public schools were effective mobility
vehicles for white American immigrant groups has been a notorious
diehard.[6] Although many want to say that the schools did assist the
various immigrants, they, in fact, did not. Most immigrants were

excluded from effective participation in the contriently interdependent competitive model of capitalism through the economic paradigm of supply and demand in labor.[7]

If A represents groups with power and B represents groups with no power, this social order can be described as one where A has power over B (A/B). Capitalism working through the contriently interdependent competitive model creates a situation where when A wins, B loses and vice versa. Inherent in the model there will always be losers. The question is not will there be unemployment, but who will be unemployed? The problem for A is how to keep B in a powerless position. The problem for B is how to achieve a position of parity and power.

Previously excluded groups formed group mobility vehicles outside the public schools for they dared not depend on A institutions contrived to promote the best interest of A. Jewish groups pulled themselves up around the synagogue and the multitude of organizations and associations protecting the Jewish community. The Irish Catholics used the Roman Catholic Church. The Chinese had the tong; the Sicilians, the Mafia. These models have been labeled power-inclusion models.[8] Such a model has five stages, the first being the separatist position wherein the groups manifest an ideology consisting of: (1) a pseudospecies declaration which articulates the belief that the group is the chosen people of God; (2) a specific identity revealed in the name the group calls itself; and (3) a territorial imperative or homeland. In the second stage, that of nationalism, the group intensifies its "we groupness" through the negative identity which provides a way to project everything bad about the group onto another people. Additionally, in this stage the ideology created in the first stage is preserved and promoted by myths, rites and rituals, associations, organizations, and finally by institutions.

This institutional development sets the stage for the kind of aggregate power which creates work niches and economic blocs. In this phase the group monopolizes some skills or controls some entry levels into unions, businesses, or other endeavors, thereby assuring members of the group easy access to the structural slots known as jobs. This economic foundation leads to stage four, or pluralism, when the group is ready to make coalitions with other groups to form voting blocs and negotiation teams on a level of parity with other groups. The last stage is the stage of power.

The serious questions now being asked regarding cultural pluralism are urgent because the groups challenging the schools have either no ideology or no alternative institutions for support. Either the public schools must do it or else. But how can one make the schools a vehicle for inclusion? If A group is alter and B group represents ego, wherein B's gratifications are contingent on its selection among available alternatives, then A's reaction will be contingent on B's selection and will result from a complementary selection on A's part. If the values and norms of A groups are the norms of all groups, this means that the schools will be used to maintain the power for A since A controls them. How can the operation of such institutions result from mindlessness when they serve to maintain power? If one rejects the argument of mindlessness, then one must face the thought that this refusal to question educational practice is a purposeful act.

If man acts for a reason, then his actions have purpose. According to Parsons and Shils, behavior is oriented to the attainment of ends or goals. Behavior takes place in situations and is normatively regulated. Additionally, it involves expenditure of energy or effort or motivation.[9] Such behaviors are called actions. Actions occur in constellations which are called systems. The schools are social systems, or systems of action, which have a process of interaction between two or more actors and where this concert is a function of collective goal orientation, or common values, and of a consensus of normative and cognitive expectations. Collective goal orientation or common values guide the choices, then, that the actors make.

Using Kluckhohn and others, a value is a conception, explicit or implicit, distinctive of an individual or characteristic of a group, of the desirable which influences the selection from available modes, means, and ends of action.[10] Values can become the large-ended goal statements of a society. Norms, standards, laws, rules, and regulations are devised to support these values or large-ended goal statements. Individuals are motivated to comply with the standards, to meet the norms, and to obey the laws, rules, and regulations. Situational factors provide the knowledge, skills, and information which motivate the individuals to comply with the norms and to obey the laws which uphold the values or large-ended goal statements. Schools are one of the many institutions which provide this knowledge and these skills and information, and values organize the systems of action.

What values organize schools? Ordinarily one thinks of achievement, respect for property, democracy, love, peace, and brotherhood. The school certainly stresses these goal statements. Why then
do certain groups fail to achieve, to respect property, and to observe
democracy, love, peace, and brotherhood? Why does the theory of
action outlined by Parsons and Shils fail to apply to public schools?
These questions create an interesting field of inquiry.

If achievement is a value, it is desirable and influences selection.
When violated, it causes guilt, shame, self-depreciation, ego diminu-
tion, or it evokes severe negative social sanctions.[11] But, in this social
order, certain groups evoke severe negative social sanctions when
they work hard. For example, black people worked in slavery from
1619 through 1865 and received nothing as remuneration, not even a
chance to run for the land when Oklahoma was opened up. The
legendary forty acres and a mule never materialized. In fact, the
emancipated blacks were returned to slavery by the deal made for a
Republican president in the First Reconstruction. Presently, black
people who graduate from college still receive less pay than whites
with high school educations.[12] Furthermore, desegregation models in
the South are displacing black teachers and creating restless new
reservoirs of black unemployment.[13]

In fact, democracy is more difficult to find no matter what definition one uses—government vested in the people or political and social
equality. Does Congress represent the poor? The young? The blacks?
Or women? Whom does Congress represent? Why do oilmen get oil
depletion allowances and some millionaires pay no income taxes?
Why are suburban homes subsidized and inner city residences "ur-
ban-renewed?" What institutions uphold the value of democracy?

Moreover, if values do not pass the tests of guilt evocation and
sanctions, are they values? Kluckhohn and others hasten to say that
one dares not assume *ex hypothesi* that verbal behavior tells the
observer less about the "true" values than other types of action, for
both verbal and nonverbal acts must be carefully studied.[14] Therefore, let us concede for the sake of the argument that achievement,
respect for property, democracy, love, peace, and brotherhood are
verbal values upheld by the norms but not characterized by conformity in action.

In fact, Wheelis argues that there are two kinds of values: institutional and instrumental. The former are derived from myths, mores,

and status and transcend the evidence at hand; the latter are derived from tool using, observation, and experimentation and are ordered by the former. If this is so, then another set of values may order, direct, organize, and integrate the values of achievement, property, love, democracy, peace, and brotherhood.[15] These institutional values may be male superiority, white European superiority, and the superiority of people with money, especially since nearly every institution in this social order and most norms, standards, laws, rules, and regulations support these three values while instantly creating three disadvantaged groups: women, blacks and non-Europeans, and the poor. Groups disadvantaged by the value system and its concomitant norms, standards, rules, regulations, and laws must change the educational system which disadvantages them.

The plain truth is that black people have inaccurate conceptual maps of reality. Another fact is that A groups (alter) control the distribution and dissemination of knowledge in order to preserve certain symbolic universes. The knowledge produced is institutionalized through certain behavior typification systems which are then internalized by individuals to maintain certain groups in excluded and/or inferior positions.

These sets of knowledge preserve the values also. America is depicted often in the curriculum as democratic but seldom as capitalistic. Since the country has not yet achieved democracy, the schools should teach the citizens the capitalistic structure so they can understand how it works and can use it to help themselves. Moreover, since food, housing, clothing, and medicine are for sale in this country at a profit, certainly the poor and the disadvantaged first should be taught how to make money. Yet, scarcely a word is said about economics except in the sense of consumership. In fact, Jules Henry states that the purpose of education is just that—to make people buy![16]

More to the point, schools where the disadvantaged are educated have programs for training in obsolete skills and trades. Few schools train or educate the poor and the disadvantaged in technology or the hard sciences. Few trade schools offer programs for apprenticeship in the building trades. More than likely, blacks are prohibited from obtaining apprenticeships. Most training for such jobs nowadays occurs on the job. The problem for blacks and women is how to get on the job!

The educational curriculum is dominated by white European feats, exploits, and miracles. Christopher Columbus discovered America even though the people he incorrectly named Indians were already here. Man began in the Caucasus Mountains, but the earliest bones of man were found in Olduvai Gorge, Kenya, East Africa. The history of the black people in America began in 1619, yet they had a homeland in Africa before that time. All kinds of European interpretations strangle black dreams and aspirations. The Constitution guarantees liberty, equality, and the pursuit of happiness. But, when blacks agitate for these guarantees, sociologists scream "rising expectations" and "benign neglect."

If culture does indeed provide the standards which are applied in evaluative processes, and if culture is an expression of a general problem—that of the relationships linking man to his environment—then B groups can no longer allow A groups to define their problems, create their values, and devise their norms. Otherwise the motivational and situational factors which work toward uniformities in codes and standards, trends in action such as striving and energy disposal, and choices and interests will continue to preserve and maintain the system of B group exclusion and cultural denigration.

A decision-making apparatus assuring B group participation and power is needed to establish a mutually shared symbolic system in the complementarity of expectations and the double contingency. This is a necessity in institutions shaping the life chances of B groups. Numerous mechanisms must be designed to afford the opportunities of a multitude of interactions among the personalities and roles within the social system of the school. These interactions act as inputs which will affect the outputs by bringing the values of the institution in line with the values of the clients.

An aggregate model is needed to accomplish these goals.[17] Such a model must give each role and group a position of parity and power in the decision making. B groups need not feel that A groups will willingly succumb or surrender these powerful institutions which keep them in power. The control of these institutions will result from repeated struggles, conflicts, and confrontations. A groups will design programs to absorb the energies of B groups and to displace the liberation goals with survival goals. A groups will co-opt B groups and B group programs so that they veer from the original directions and point toward A group goals and ends. This is to be expected since A groups are in power. However, the struggle must go on. The change will be effective if the values are no longer acknowledged and/or respected. Alternate symbolic universes will be legitimatized if the people so decide.

Such a school which is a vehicle for cultural pluralism would operate from an aggregate model rather than a specialization model. One such model is CAPTS,[18] designed and implemented in the Wood-lawn Experimental Schools District Project (WESP), an Elementary and Secondary Education Act (ESEA), Title III government-funded project under Public Law 89-10 in Chicago. This project is operated under a tripartite arrangement with three institutions: the Woodlawn Organization, the University of Chicago, and the Chicago Board of Education. The district is governed by the Woodlawn Community Board which has twenty-one members, ten from the Woodlawn Organization, seven from the Chicago Board of Education, and four from the University of Chicago. The Woodlawn Community Board makes policy for the district. However, it is only a recommending body as the Chicago Board of Education retains approval-veto powers.

The district, located in Woodlawn, one of the ten poorest of the seventy-five city community areas, has three components: the community component, the research and evaluation component, and the in-school component. It has three schools: Hyde Park High School, Wadsworth Elementary School, and Wadsworth Upper Grade Center. The community component has twenty-five community agents who organize and convene some forty parent councils of approximately twenty members each. These parent councils each elect a president or chairman who sits on the Woodlawn Parent Council Advisory Board. These members become alternates for Woodlawn Community Board members. These parent council presidents attend leadership training sessions to learn how to be a board member, how to use *Robert's Rules of Order,* and how to understand school law, board rules, and other necessary information.

The in-school component has forty community teachers (teachers' aides). These community teachers and parents attend workshops in methods of teaching the Ethnolinguistic Cultural Approach to Oral Language and the Sensory-Motor-Perceptual Program. Community teachers have learned to test and screen for the latter program, and many of them know how to teach the first rudiments of reading skills. Moreover, parents have been trained for positions as community agents, community teachers, and research assistants, and they serve in classrooms on teams to solve problems.

The primary objective of the WESP is to restructure the social system through a mutuality of effort by subsequent interventions which have two focuses: (1) to change the roles and relationships in the school and (2) to change the roles and relationships in the community. The project is not only interested in who works together, but how. To the degree that the mutuality of effort effects a restructuring of the social system, the following secondary objectives are to be achieved: (1) elevation of achievement scores, (2) an improvement in self-concept, (3) a reduction in alienation, and (4) a sense of power over one's destiny. Mutuality of effort was to be achieved through CAPTS, and the CAPTS-WESP decision-making model was to be the vehicle to restructure the social system and to produce cultural pluralism in WESP.

The model has nine steps (see Figure 4-1). Program planning occurs in the CAPTS Congress. First, each group meets separately. A plan emerges from a group. It is submitted to the other groups, which discuss and negotiate. The negotiated plan is then sent to the professional bureaucracy to be formulated into an educational program. This formulation is sent to the administrative staff for organization. The administrative staff then submits the proposal to the Woodlawn Community Board (WCB). The WCB recommends or does not recommend. If WCB recommends and the proposal does not warrant submission to the Chicago Board of Education (CBE) (this means it does not infringe upon the power of the CBE), the proposal then comes back to the administrative staff for coordination and communication, to the professional bureaucracy for implementation, and back to the CAPTS Congress for evaluation. Each group first meets separately to discuss the method and the instruments to be used for evaluation. These are then negotiated, and the evaluation takes place according to the negotiated plan. If a proposal or plan fails to be recommended by the WCB or is vetoed by the CBE, it returns to the CAPTS Congress and starts over again.

Implementing cultural pluralism demands the input which an aggregate model provides. It needs the diagnostic skills of the professional staff. In such a school, diagnosis would be the important program. Teachers would need to become skilled in techniques of data collection and analysis, such as interviewing, microethnography,

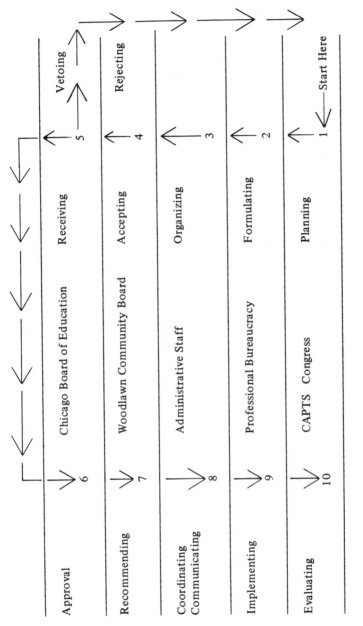

Figure 4-1. Community control decision-making model

questionnaire construction, public opinion polling, test construction, categorizing, and codification. Diagnosis would not stop or necessarily start in the classroom but would encompass the entire community, especially as it related to the student's present, past, and future existence. It would need administrators amenable to the collective decision-making model described above or administrators willing to share power.

More important, excluded groups cannot conform to A group's system of "ways of orienting," and B groups must project their new external symbols to control new ways of orienting so that the new system will be geared into the action systems of both A and B. The construction and maintenance of the public school system is far from mindless. It is purposeful, directed toward the preservation of B group's conformity to A group's norms and values.

To make the schools a vehicle for cultural pluralism, the institutional values of male superiority, white European superiority, and the superiority of people with money must be abandoned. Secondly, education must be for the purpose of self-fulfillment and self-realization by the expansion of the human potential for the best possible interests of each person concerned so that he can lead a more meaningful life in a democracy for the betterment of himself and all mankind.

Next, a new all-human ethic must be employed. One that could be tried is that of the "Golden Talent." The basic assumption is that people are different. Each person is predisposed toward a certain approach to learning. Some people are sight learners; some, kinesthetic; some, auditory; some are abstract thinkers; some manipulate ideas; some memorize. In fact, there may be as many approaches to learning as there are people. But everyone has a talent. Observations of these will dictate what is taught to that learner. This curriculum will not be obstructed by racist and/or chauvinist values.

There is no doubt that a democratic culturally pluralistic society is imperative. That fights must be waged on all fronts is accepted. Let Americans tell no more lies, make no more myths, create no more evasions like integration and desegregation, revenue sharing and voucher systems. At long last, let's set about to cure the disease and not treat the symptoms. Education can be concerned then with the meeting of men's needs of identity, stimulation, and security based on the values of land, liberty, and life. Once this occurs, the vital area of man's purpose and existence on this earth becomes the primary focus of his educational experience and the point position at the frontier of knowledge.

Notes

1. Charles E. Silberman, *Crisis in the Classroom* (New York: Random House, 1970).

2. Sekou Toure, "A Dialectical Approach to Culture," *Black Scholar* 1 (November 1969), 13.

3. The following discussion of culture was taken from Talcott Parsons and Edward A. Shils (eds.), *Toward a General Theory of Action* (New York: Harper and Row, 1951), 14-16.

4. Harold Cruse, *The Crisis of the Negro Intellectual* (New York: William Morrow, 1967), 456.

5. See Talcott Parsons, "Full Citizenship Rights for the Negro," in Talcott Parsons and Kenneth B. Clark (eds.), *The Negro American* (Boston: Houghton Mifflin, 1965), 720-22.

6. Silberman, *op. cit.*, 54-58.

7. Morton Deutsch defines "contrient interdependence" as "the condition in which individuals are so linked together that there is a negative correlation between their goal attainments." For a discussion of the contriently interdependent model, see Morton Deutsch, "Cooperation and Trust: Some Theoretical Notes," in Warren G. Bennis *et al.* (eds.), *Interpersonal Dynamics* (Homewood, Illinois: Dorsey Press, 1964), 564-82.

8. Barbara A. Sizemore, "Separatism: A Reality Approach to Inclusion?" in Robert L. Green (ed.), *Racial Crisis in American Education* (Chicago: Follett Educational Corporation, 1969), 249-79.

9. Parsons and Shils, *op. cit.*, 53.

10. Clyde Kluckhohn *et al.*, "Values and Value-Orientations in the Theory of Action: An Exploration in Definition and Classification," in Parsons and Shils, *op. cit.*, 395.

11. *Ibid.*, 407-408.

12. Thomas Johnson, "Returns from Investment in Human Capital," *American Economic Review* 60 (September 1970), 558.

13. Robert Hooker, "Integration Cheats Black Teachers," *Chicago Sun-Times*, January 10, 1971, sec. 2, 2-3.

14. Kluckhohn *et al., op. cit.*, 406.

15. Allen Wheelis, *The Quest for Identity* (New York: W. W. Norton, 1958), 179. See also Barbara A. Sizemore, "Social Science and the Black Identity," in James A. Banks and Jean D. Grambs (eds.), *Black Self-Concept* (New York: McGraw-Hill, 1971).

16. Jules Henry, *Culture against Man* (New York: Random House, 1963).

17. Morris Janowitz, "Institution Building in Urban Education," in David

Street (ed.), *Innovations in Mass Education* (New York: John Wiley, 1969), 273-342.

18. CAPTS: Community representative Administrators, Parents, Teachers, and Students.

5. Community Control: The Values behind a Call for Change

Judson Hixson

Historically the American public school system has been based on the ideal that all of the children of all of the people with their many different degrees of motivation can be and are to be accommodated.[1] This principle, however, has never actually been practiced in American public schools, or, for that matter, in higher education. The reality is that in America public education has been based primarily on the culture of the white middle class and on racial ethnocentrism. Thus, minority groups throughout the country have had to attempt cultural and educational isolation in an effort to maintain cultural survival. This phenomenon is even truer of some other minorities than of black Americans.

In recent years, however, America has been witnessing the semblance of a trend toward restructuring its educational practices, a trend based on multicultural elements, in an effort to resolve some of its social ills. Community control has been one of the proposed schemes for this restructuring. This study of the concept of community control emphasizes some of the cultural and value orientations that lie behind it.

An Origin in Culture

In *Crisis in the Classroom* Charles Silberman makes the point that education is the product of American society and culture, and is the deliberate and purposeful creation, evocation, or transmission of knowledge, abilities, skills, and values.[2]

In criticizing Silberman's analysis, Barbara Sizemore notes that he mistakenly cites mindlessness as the causal factor behind the problems in public schools. Defining mindlessness as the failure either to think seriously about education or to question established practice, Silberman's analysis completely avoids discussions of "purposeful action" and thereby eliminates examination of forceful cultural imperatives such as racism.[3] He concludes correctly, however, that the idea of the public schools as effective mobility vehicles, even for white American immigrant groups, is little more than a "notoriously diehard myth."[4] If we then accept the premise that mindlessness cannot be judged the major cause of today's problems in education, we must look for other explanations of actions that have led to systematic educational neglect of black Americans.

Schools are among the several institutions that provide the knowledge, skills, information, and values that organize various systems of action. What values, then, guide the schools? "Ordinarily one thinks of achievement, respect for property, democracy, love, peace and brotherhood?"[5] The question now becomes: Why do certain groups fail to achieve, to respect property, and to observe democracy, love, peace, and brotherhood? Are there institutional values which operate to limit applicability of these "universal" values to some subgroups of the total population?

In America such discriminatory institutional values include racial superiority, sexual superiority, and financial superiority. This is particularly evident when we consider that virtually every social institution in this society, as well as most norms, standards, laws, rules, regulations, and the like, support whites of European background, males, and the wealthy, thereby creating three disadvantaged groups: blacks and non-Europeans, women, and the poor.[6]

Such a definition of the problem precludes recommendations for voucher programs, revenue sharing, right-to-read programs, differentiated staffing, self-concept development programs, male-model projects, "instant Negro" faculty members, forced integration, performance contracts, open classrooms, and other reform movements. If the value system itself is creating the problem, then a real revolution is in order. Groups disadvantaged by the value system and its concomitant norms, standards, rules, regulations, and laws must change the system that disenfranchises them.

The educational system provides information, skills, and knowledge for those who control it. Evidence clearly points to the failure of the schools insofar as blacks and non-Europeans and the poor are concerned. Black students in particular continue to be at the bottom of the barrel when test scores are published.

Recently some social scientists have gone even further in their support of racist and chauvinistic values. Arthur Jensen has made attempts to assign blacks to inferior genetic groups with I.Q. tests.[7] Edward C. Banfield supports the white European culture as the "normal" culture, the most profound motivating dynamic being future orientation.[8] Coleman found that poor children are positively affected by the affluence of their classmates.[9] Pettigrew and others argued that blacks could learn better in schools with whites.[10] Such studies further perpetrate the institutional values already cited. No significant change will occur in the schools until a new value system is designed and implemented, based on land, liberty, and life.

If culture does indeed provide the standards which are applied in evaluative processes, and if culture is an expression of the general problem of the relationships linking man to his environment, then minority groups can no longer allow dominant groups to define their problems, create their values, and devise their norms, much less evaluate their cultural standards.

It is in this light that our discussion now shifts to the idea of community control as one possible apparatus for creating a symbolic universe for minority peoples that will serve their interests and values, and prepare them for participation in, not manipulation by, America's social system.

Community Control

Increasing attention is currently being given to the problems of culturally different minority populations as they relate to the formal educational process. The purpose of this section is to distinguish the concept of the culturally different[11] from the culturally "disadvantaged" pupil, and to explore some of the other values which the monocultural orientation of schools in the United States suggests. A possible remedy in the form of regionally relevant, that is, community-controlled, schools is advocated.

The field of education of cultural minorities is indeed a complex one, with pertinent and some not so pertinent data being produced by research in education, anthropology, sociology, social psychology, and other areas. Understandably, a tremendous variety of viewpoints can be found among parents, students, practicing educators, and scholars, ranging from favoring white-controlled, monocultural, assimilationist programs to minority-controlled, monocultural, anti-assimilationist programs.[12] We turn now to a discussion of some of the reasons for advocating community control of schools, and later to an elaboration of one of the crucial psychological factors motivating people toward the concept of community control.

The minority group dealt with will be primarily black Americans. This group has been subjected to the most devastating and systematic dehumanizing and racist experiences in all areas of American society, not the least of which is education. The movement toward community control of big-city schools has been one of the most recent controversial developments in education. Black Americans have demanded the power to govern those schools that "serve" black students.

The demand for community control of schools can only be understood by recognizing the frustrations that blacks and other racial minorities have experienced in their quest for freedom, equality, and dignity through the educative process. Two hundred years of slavery have been followed by one hundred years of "freedom," and the black American still remains outside the mainstream of American life. By all standards and measures, his welfare is substantially below that of white Americans. Statistics on unemployment, life expectancy, housing, and infant mortality all reflect his unenviable position. Massive discrimination in both governmental and private sectors have prevented any semblance of equal rights for the black man. While recent attempts have allegedly begun to redress these inequities, progress has been pitifully slow, if evident at all.

Yet the worst condition facing the American black man has been his feeling of powerlessness, his lack of a feeling of legitimacy and personal worth. He is imprisoned in overpriced housing in the ghetto, and his choice of jobs is limited. He does not have residential or occupational mobility; nor does he have the political power to counter these disabling conditions.[13] His feelings of impotence have, moreover, been compounded by the failure of those social institutions designed to "improve" his lot and his future prospects.

Thus, the basic problem of the black American is to gain control over his destiny. In recent years a prospective solution has come into focus. Through a program of racial cohesiveness and self-development, the black man intends to liberate himself from racism and to gain equality and dignity. Foremost in this drive is the quest to redirect and reform those institutions that have failed black Americans or, worse, have inflicted injury and further disadvantaged black and other racial minorities. In black neighborhoods in big cities the schools have been the first institutions challenged.

Neither urban educators nor informed laymen dispute that city schools have failed to help the black American substantially improve his status. This indictment of the schools is particularly serious because it is the formal educational process that represents the primary social device for equalizing opportunities among children of different races and social groupings. Yet, while 75 percent of white males in their late twenties have completed high school, only about 60 percent of nonwhite males in this category have received a high school education.

The black American, then, enters his adult life with severe educational deficiencies, and the nature of the schooling experience that is provided for him must share a large portion of the blame for this condition. The average black in the large city attends a school that is less well endowed than that attended by whites. Yet inferior resources are only one way in which the schools hamper the preparation of the ghetto child for a productive life.

More destructive to his self-concept and growth is the cultural intolerance reflected in his school experience. The materials, curriculum, and teaching methods, as well as basic value orientations were developed for the white middle-class child and are, as they have been historically, largely irrelevant to the experiences and special educational requirements of the black child. Thus, the present schools in black neighborhoods undermine the identity of the black student by ignoring his cultural heritage and sense of legitimacy. The big city schools have, in effect, forced the black student to be a captive audience in a hostile environment—one that does not consider his needs. In this sense the schools definitely do not reflect the pluralism that is claimed by our society.

Since blacks intend to take responsibility for those institutions that mold their lives, it is no accident that the schools represent the initial focal point. As a participant in a recent conference has pointed out, the natural and logical vehicle for a first thrust would understandably be the schools. They are present, constant, and, further, they represent the "white underbelly" of society. Unlike political administrators who often function out of a back room in city hall, the administrators of the schools are present, as are the teachers. Schools, therefore, represent a tangible vehicle around which action can focus.[14] In addition to the visibility of the schools, there is the widespread impression that, in the long run, education is a potent force in society and that those who control it control something that is very important.

The conventional thinking of the late 1950's and early 1960's suggested that, through racially integrating the schools, the educational problems of blacks and other racial minorities would be solved. The failure, however, of big-city school boards to deliver what they promised produced much of the present distrust of centralized school boards on the part of minority citizens. Even the U.S. Commission on Civil Rights found that "many black students who attend majority white schools are in fact in majority black classrooms.[15] Many blacks reject integration as a solution not only because it is identified with false promises, but also because it has ideological overtones that affront black dignity. As Floyd McKissick has suggested, the view that quality education can take place only in an integrated setting seems to be based on the degrading proposition: "Mix Negroes with Negroes and you get stupidity."

A second approach to improving schools in the ghettos has been called compensatory education. During the early 1960's it became the vogue for educators to refer to the educationally "deprived" or the educationally "disadvantaged" child. Most urban blacks were considered disadvantaged because they lacked the home and community environment that stimulated white-defined educational motivation and achievement and produced white middle-class values and attitudes. Additional school resources were to be provided to help the "disadvantaged" child "make up" or compensate for his deficiencies. The record to date, however, has been unimpressive. The same teachers, curriculum, school organization, educational methods, and philosophies that have consistently failed the ghetto child have largely been retained, and little educational progress has been shown.

It is clear that the schools as presently constituted have shown little evidence of being able to fulfill the educational needs of the "disadvantaged" child, particularly the black child. Both compensatory education and integration have witnessed more failures than successes, and all of the future programs for improving the education of black children revolve around one or both of these approaches. In a sense, the representatives of the black community are telling professional educators and the white community: "You have had your chance, and our schools are no better. Blacks now demand the chance to solve their own educational problems," and the professionals have not been able to counter these demands with any new alternatives. Instead the response has been along the line: "Just give us a chance to provide racially integrated, quality education." Moreover, recent decisions by the U.S. Supreme Court as well as proclamations from Washington, most notably from the executive branch, have all served to indicate that little if any desire exists among those in power to push for meaningful changes in the education of black Americans. This becomes particularly evident if proposed changes might "upset" a politician's white constituency.

The surge for self-determination combined with the failure of professionals to prove themselves has made the schools particularly vulnerable, a vulnerability manifested in the increasingly voiced sentiment that the education of blacks can no longer be considered the "white man's burden." The black community has rejected this approach with its paternalistic overtones; it now wants to take the responsibility for the schooling of its own.

As mentioned earlier, the general reaction of educators to the problem of underachievement, alienation, and withdrawal as it relates to racial and cultural minorities has been to intensify the use of traditional approaches and to focus the "blame" for failure on the minority group. The concepts of culturally "disadvantaged" and "deprived" youth have been coined and serve to suggest that the minority student and his family are at fault and that the pupil and his subculture should be manipulated. The traditional system is, in effect, a finished product that serves majority students well. It should not, therefore, be seriously challenged. Minority groups must adjust, must conform. Since the schools and programs remain and are considered basically sound, there is no need for fundamental revision. As Reginald W. Major, a former chairman of the Educational Committee of the San Francisco NAACP, has noted, "By accepting the premise of cultural deprivation, school administrators and school boards delude themselves into believing that special programs designed to compensate for an inadequate home environment are all that is needed."[16]

Operation Headstart, the National Teacher's Corps, and compensatory education programs are generally based on the assumption that increased exposure to any school environment coupled with an intense remedial approach will solve any problems of the culturally "deprived."

It may be that those who are serious about wanting to improve the educational situation of the "disadvantaged" child will have to take a new, closer look to see which end of the pupil-teacher continuum is really disadvantaged. Jack Forbes asks, "Are 'disadvantaged' pupils attending 'advantaged' schools taught by 'culturally enriched' teachers, or is it possible that some culturally 'different' pupils are more enriched than their culturally 'deprived' teachers and schools, or are all deprived . . . schools, pupils, and teachers?"[17]

Cultural deprivation is not a new concept. For at least a century it has been an expression of white America's racism, chauvinism, and belief in its own superiority. The concept of cultural deprivation as it has frequently been used is simply a belief that nonwhite minority groups do not possess a culture that can be enhanced by the schools. The children of minority groups are "deprived" because they are not carriers of the white middle-class heritage, and the task of the schools is to make up for this deficiency. Or, to put it another way, the school is used as a device for assimilation, that is, making the United States into a nation of multihued white Americans.[18]

Cultural deprivation, in short, is not merely an insult to black Americans. It is a continuation of the missionary urge of White Anglo-Saxon Protestants (WASPs) to demonstrate the alleged superiority of their culture by attempting to make everyone else over in their image. Is this not merely a form of cultural imperialism made possible by the sheer economic and political dominance of the white American majority?

Educators seem often to operate in a mythical world created by the nature of their own middle-class contacts and experiences. Having little to do with low-income or nonwhite people generally, they assume that persons possessing white middle-class skills and values will, in effect, function successfully at every level of life. Because the educator fails to suspect that it may be his culture that is regionally irrelevant and alien, he continually attempts to train young blacks to be middle-class whites, at the same time denying most black men and women the ability to make a living in such a social context.

It is naïve to assume that the majority of black Americans will spend most of their lives in a middle-class setting. Urban or rural, the average black is going to continue to be living in an essentially black culture, in both sociological and economic terms.

The educator who seeks to train the young black must not ignore the realities of black American life and, above all, he must not regard the black American subculture as simply a tragic but temporary inconvenience to be gradually eliminated. Ultimately the black community as a whole will have more to say about this question than any group of educators, black or white.

More telling than any other argument, however, is the fact that middle-class whites have prevailed for at least a century. What is needed today is not more of the same in greater doses, but a completely different conception of the school and of its relationship to cultural heterogeneity. Nathaniel Hickerson, in *Education for Alienation,* points out that the affluent orientation of most teachers in American society makes it difficult, if not impossible, for them to understand or cope with the behavior of children from economically deprived families. He goes on to state that this clash of value commitments more than anything else is responsible for driving minority students out of the schools and into the street. They have been attacked at the point of greatest vulnerability, their own value structure.[19] Dr. Eleanor Leacock of the Brooklyn Polytechnic Institute, after completing a study of slum education, reported that this same misunderstanding was largely responsible for the staggering inequalities found in the New York Public Schools.[20]

The unicultural school in America is not just alien to many regions and communities in terms of cultural reality; it also may well serve as the major cause of tensions that thwart the avowed educational goals of the school and at the same time produce alumni unfitted for participation in any culture.

Legitimacy: An Organizing Dimension

It has already been noted that the development of a black self-concept, an identity awareness, is one of the motivating factors behind the drive toward community control. Coupled inseparably with the idea of a self-concept is the idea of legitimacy—one's belief in himself as a legitimate person, as a worthwhile being. This final section gives some of the psychological constructs behind the relationship of legitimacy to the public school system.

Partly by design and partly by accident, the public school system contributes to the organization of social life through its promotion of values and concepts common to a given set of human experiences. Value orientations are promoted through the articulation of social goals worth striving for and through the reinforcement of certain behavioral means used in such striving. Conceptual orientations, on the other hand, are created and indeed maintained by the very process of social communication. This process of communication is inherent in the educational process. It both transmits and provides notions of "what exists," "what is important," and "what is related to what else."[21]

Schools are unique from other socializing agencies, however, in that efforts to create behavioral structure are more deliberate and thorough. The typical child spends a larger portion of his formative years in schools than in any other single social institution.

The self-concept is conceived of here in a literal fashion, the conception a person has of himself. A conception is a belief, and beliefs are the fundamental elements of psychological systems. By a "system" is meant a collection of beliefs in dynamic interaction, and the self system is the collection of interacting beliefs that a person has about himself.

The self system contains two distinct sets of beliefs or "subsystems." One set concerns the self as actor; the other set concerns the self as acted upon.[22] While some theorists find this dual conception of the self limiting, it seems to be quite useful in that it provides a foundation for the analysis of black-white interactions. As a preliminary to the later discussion of the idea of legitimacy, it will be helpful to consider various aspects of the first subsystem, that dealing with the self as an actor, the psychological base of which is the idea of competency. Without this understanding the idea of legitimacy may seem to exist in a vacuum.

It was Robert White who first brought attention to the psychological significance of competency. He defined competency as "an organism's capacity to interact effectively with its environment."[23] Aside from obvious successes that man has had in controlling his physical environment, he has also had a dramatic effect on his social environment. This effect manifests itself in the high degree of predictability that *seems* to characterize human behavior. Thus social organizations seem to be the highest form of demonstrated competency. The ability to predict human behavior is tremendously aided by the use of perceptible differences (for example, racial differences) as principles of social organization. In any case, Professor Cedric Clark of Stanford University has noted that man has organized his systems of social interactions, and this organization is both a consequence of and a contribution to psychological competency.

A direct consequence of this organizing of social interactions is the psychological assignment, sometimes overassignment, of social roles. In considering the development and maintenance of the black self concept, it is important to emphasize the role of culture in sustaining role expectations. What seems to be significant, Clark asserts, is the extent to which the culture of the white middle-aged male constitutes a behavioral "program" for all individuals in our social system.

The following quotation from Goffman is relevant:

... in an important sense there is only one complete unblushing male in America: a young, married, white, urban, northern, heterosexual, Protestant father of college education, fully employed, of good complexion, weight and height, and a recent record in sports. Every American male tends to look out at the world from this perspective, thus constituting one sense in which one can speak of a common value system in America ... "[24]

This dominant culture contains the values and concepts which are used to define, assess, and account for the decision-making activities of almost all other Americans. This is not to say that Goffman's image is the only one transmitting values and concepts, but it does seem to be the dominant one presented most frequently in our educational institutions and the institutions of mass communication.

A concept is a convenient label, the function or usefulness of which can be assessed only in relation to the environment in which a particular individual operates. To be more explicit, concepts which are not descriptive of or relevant to the environment in which a group of people live are not learned as easily as those which are both descriptive and relevant. To the extent that the institutions of education, or, more exactly, the process of education, are more or less uniform in terms of communication content manifested (for example, texts), and to the extent that the transmission of concepts and values is basic to all communication, it would seem that the concepts that are transmitted are related to some restricted set of experiences. As Clark points out, many educators are beginning to realize that the "Dick and Jane" reading series, for example, is totally alien to the life experiences of most ghetto children. What is not often considered, however, is the fact that the feeling of incompetency characterizing many blacks may be directly related to failure experiences resulting from their being tested with these foreign concepts. It is interesting to note that, as early as 1949, Allison Davis pointed out this same idea of culturally biased testing.[25]

As mentioned previously, concepts are man-made labels. They are used in the codification of a given domain of reality. In the social arena this given domain is the human social experience. And, since the experiences of individuals differ, the concepts used in the communication of this reality are likely to be different.

It would seem to follow, then, that the people best qualified to assess competency with regard to the acquisition and utilization of concepts, which constitutes learning, would be those who participate in the culture created by shared life experiences. It is in this context that the concern for community-controlled schools—whether predominantly white or black—has a firm social-psychological base. The advantage of an integrated school seems to lie, theoretically, in its ability to expand a student's store of concepts by exposing him to a set different from his own. What is defined as school integration, however, most often does not attempt to do this. What typically happens is that black students are expected to learn concepts associated with the white culture, but there are no reciprocal expectations with respect to whites. Further, the learning abilities of black students are usually evaluated in terms of their ability to master such white concepts. This is one of the major expectations of behavior that black students are currently attempting to redefine.

The concept of the self was previously defined as a dual, stressing the self as both actor and object. Thus, we have the self consisting of two sets of beliefs: one set dealing with the belief that one's actions are, have been, and will be competent; the other dealing with the belief that the definition and conception of oneself by others is a worthy one. According to Muzafer Sherif, the interrelated attitudes that the individual has acquired about himself and others "define and regulate his relatedness to them in concrete situations and activities."[26] This definition and regulation may be regarded as reflecting the individual's "legitimacy." Beliefs about legitimacy may be regarded as dependent upon the extent to which a person feels recognized and respected.

The importance of recognition should not be underestimated, particularly as it relates to nonwhite (and nonmale) individuals. By not recognizing individuals we decrease their social worth and significance, and this is exactly what has been done to black Americans as a group. Themes of black creative writing, for example, have dealt with the idea of nonrecognition. James Baldwin claims that *Nobody Knows My Name.*[27] Ralph Ellison speaks of an *Invisible Man.*[28] And black children talk about *The Me Nobody Knows.*[29]

While the process of recognition is necessary for legitimation to occur, it is not sufficient. An additional condition is the feeling that one is respected. One has this feeling when he believes that others share his definition of reality, judge his behavior fairly, and attribute his achievements to himself and his failures to his environment.[30]

When incompetence is attributed to personal characteristics (for example, "Black students fail because black people are inherently incapable of success."), or competency is attributed to external causes (for example, "Black students can succeed if the environment is enriched."), the black student may be said to be "delegitimated." This process has quite often been used against black Americans, and it constitutes the basis of what has been termed "racism."

When one suggests that the black American has not been recognized, it is not proposed that what is missing is black-white interaction. The process is more subtle than that and usually occurs at a cultural level. It is not a lack of face-to-face contact, but a lack of culture-to-culture interaction. From this perspective, then, it is not people that need to be integrated, but rather ideas, values, and concepts. A problem arises, however, in that some observers have questioned the very existence of a black culture.

Returning to the idea of respect as a component of the legitimation process, it will be recalled that a person's self-concept tends to be confirmed to the extent that his definition of reality is respected. School systems often unconsciously disconfirm or delegitimate the black self-concept by failing to acknowledge or explore the realities of the black experience. This is often done by presenting as friends of the black community those very persons defined as enemies by blacks themselves. When this is done by the schools, it is termed propaganda, as these types of socialization activities deviate too far from the black reality.

In addition to the idea of recognition and respect, an individual also needs feedback on the nature of his behavior. Clark notes that it is important for such feedback to occur, and that it not be restricted solely to positive or negative evaluations. It is a common observation that much of the behavioral assessment of the black school child is negative. Such evaluations instill in the child feelings of delegitimation or personal unworth.

The reason white Americans have been sources for black legitimation has nothing to do with the fact that they are white. A white source of legitimation is needed because it is the white culture that guides the operation of major social institutions within which black behavior is defined, assessed, and regulated. Conversely, the reason blacks have not been able to rely on other blacks for legitimation is because black concepts and values are not manifested in dominant institutions. Thus, those who display competence and power, especially the power to define social reality, become, for better or worse, sources of legitimation. It is this power that blacks are striving for in their demands for community-relevant and community-controlled schools. If blacks cannot make their values a major part of the dominant culture, they can at least control the legitimation processes in the educational institutions that so profoundly affect the children in their charge.

Notes

1. E. Sekaquaptewa, "Community as a Product of Education for Cultural Pluralism: Conformal Education vs. Mutual Respect," in M. D. Stent, W. R. Hazard, and H. N. Rivlin (eds.), *Cultural Pluralism in Education* (New York: Appleton-Century-Crofts, 1972), 35.

2. Charles E. Silberman, *Crisis in the Classroom* (New York: Random House, 1970), 5-6.

3. See Chapter 4.

4. Silberman, *op. cit.*, 53-56.

5. See Chapter 4.

6. *Ibid.*

7. Arthur Jensen, "How Much Can We Boost I.Q. and Scholastic Achievement?" *Harvard Educational Review* 39 (February 1969), 1-123.

8. Edward C. Banfield, *The Unheavenly City* (Boston: Little, Brown and Co., 1970).

9. James S. Coleman, *Equality of Educational Opportunity* (Washington, D. C.: U. S. Government Printing Office, 1966).

10. United States Commission on Civil Rights, *Racial Isolation in the Public Schools* (Washington, D.C.: U. S. Government Printing Office, 1967).

11. J. Forbes, *Education of the Culturally Different—A Multi-Cultural Approach* (Washington, D. C.: U.S. Government Printing Office, 1968).

12. *Ibid.*

13. Cedric Clark, "Competency and Legitimacy as Organizing Dimensions in the Black Self-Concept," unpublished manuscript, 1971.

14. H. Levin, "Introduction," in H. Levin (ed.), *Community Control of Schools* (Washington, D. C.: Brookings Institution, 1970), 6.

15. United States Commission on Civil Rights, *op. cit.*, Vol. I.

16. *The Nation,* September 12, 1966.

17. Forbes, *op. cit.*

18. *Ibid.*

19. Nathaniel Hickerson, *Education for Alienation* (Englewood Cliffs, New Jersey: Prentice-Hall, 1966).

20. *New York Times,* November 19, 1966.

21. Clark, *op. cit.*

22. *Ibid.*

23. Robert White, "Motivation Reconsidered: The Concept of Competence," *Psychological Review* 66 (1959), 297-334.

24. E. Goffman, *Stigma: Notes on the Management of Spoiled Identity* (Englewood Cliffs, New Jersey: Prentice-Hall, 1963), 128.

25. Allison Davis and Kenneth Eells, *Intelligence and Cultural Differences* (Chicago: University of Chicago Press, 1951).

26. Clark, *op. cit.*

27. James Baldwin, *Nobody Knows My Name* (New York: Dial Press, 1961).

28. Ralph Ellison, *Invisible Man* (New York: Random House, 1952).

29. S. Joseph (ed.), *The Me Nobody Knows: Childrens' Voices from the Ghetto* (New York: Avon Books, 1969).

30. Clark, *op. cit.*

6. The Utilization of Behavioral and Social Sciences in Minority Group Education

Some Critical Implications

Edward J. Barnes

The Problem

It is almost a cliché today to state that the American educational system has largely failed in its efforts to educate the children of oppressed minority groups. Academic achievement on the average is consistently found lagging behind grade expectancy. The tendency to fall behind appears as early as the first grade and intensifies as the child moves through the upper grades. By the sixth grade, the average young inner-city dweller has fallen behind approximately three grades in mathematics and reading. The schools, as representatives of the larger society, virtually ignore the values of these groups, while embracing the perspective of the "white Anglo-Saxon Ideal." Thus, there appears to be a direct relationship between the degree to which a group's values, norms, and standards are excluded from the dominant values of the society, and the failure of the society's schools to educate its members. Apparently, the schools, as subsystems of the larger societal system, reflect the dominant trends of the society, vis-à-vis its powerless minorities.

This paper was presented at the annual meeting of the American Psychological Association, Washington, D. C., September 1971.

Over the past several years, particularly with the advent of the "War on Poverty" concept, increased attention has been given to this grave national problem. Numerous programs ("educational enrichment," "demonstration," "compensatory," "Pilot," among others) have been undertaken, but for the most part these efforts have not produced sustained improvement in the skills of reading and mathematics.[1]

If this is the case, at least three questions must be asked: What specifically do the behavioral and social sciences have to contribute currently to the explanation and resolution of the problem? What potentially do they have to contribute? What factors might hinder or facilitate maximum future contributions?

Theoretical Explanations of Underachievement in Minority Groups

With respect to the first question it is clear that, while the persistent and cumulative educational underachievement of students in large inner-city areas is conceded, there is no consensus as to cause or remedy. Most currently offered theoretical explanations tend to locate the causal factors within the child and his family, while excluding or minimizing the schools and other institutions as determinants. The theories offered in explanation of underachievement in this group can be subsumed under five categories: biological or racial, physiological, demographic, psychological, and sociological.

Biological or Racial Explanations

The biological or racial explanations have probably been around the longest. They are periodically brought forward to explain differences between members of the majority and those of oppressed minority groups and to justify practices that maintain the minorities in positions of subjugation, a notable example being the status of slavery.[2] These explanations, in their crude and sophisticated forms, are racist in their assertion that black and other oppressed minority children on the average achieve below whites because of genetic inferiority to whites. Whatever one thinks of these explanations, they cannot be ignored because they are part of the fabric of American history and they are consistent with the contemporary pattern of racism. Consequently such explanations have considerable potential influence on people in powerful policy-making positions. A unique feature of these explanations is that they do not provide for any form of external or postnatal manipulation to prevent academic retardation or to increase individual achievement. Explanations within this framework, as exemplified by A. R. Jensen[3] in his assessment of the national Head Start effort, assert that compensatory educational programs will not work and that desegregation will not work; they imply that nothing short of biological control (eugenics) can be effective.

Numerous criticisms can be invoked against the validity of these theories, ranging from those that are obvious, such as the flaws in the definitions of race utilized, to more analytic criticisms, as exemplified by C. A. Valentine.[4] He asserts that any theory of class or racial deficits of biological origin is undemonstrable and scientifically untestable in an ethnically plural and structurally discriminatory society. The necessary separation of biological and sociocultural factors is methodologically impossible in such a setting. Kenneth Clark[5] points out a most obvious flaw not previously highlighted, namely, that these theories do not explain the fact that low-income white students in the south and in urban public schools are also, on the average, consistently retarded in academic subjects.

Physiological Explanations

Physiological theories which focus on neurological and sensory deficiencies assert that the academic retardation of these children is a consequence of the by-products of poverty and deprivation. Hilda Knoblock and Benjamin Pasamanick have been leaders in the study of brain and neurological defects resulting from prenatal and postnatal malnutrition.[6] Obviously this theory will explain academic retardation in some cases. There is evidence, however, that even in extreme cases of obvious mental retardation and organic brain damage, when such children are taught in a supportive educational situation by teachers who accept them, they make striking gains, both educational and personal.[7] There is danger in attributing academic retardation among oppressed minority group children to physiological causes in view of the prevalence of educational underachievement in this group and the present ambiguity in the diagnosis of mental deficiencies. It is a simple matter to substitute physiological deficit for genetic inferiority in day-to-day operations. In either case, low academic achievement is viewed as irremediable.

Demographic Explanations

Demographic theories emphasize where children live and go to school in explaining their educational achievement. James S. Coleman found that the academic performance of black youngsters increased after attending a previously all white school.[8] Otto Klineberg found that black youngsters born in the northern part of the U.S. scored higher on I.Q. tests than did their newly arrived counterparts from the southern part of the country.[9] However, the differential tended to wash out over time, as the southern-born youngsters remained in the North, apparently reflecting the positive influence of the northern setting. Thus, it is asserted that large numbers of lower-status children, whose families migrated from southern to northern states, brought with them the consequences of segregated and inferior education.[10] If this were the controlling factor, one would expect a direct, positive relation between length of time in the "better schools" and increase in academic achievement. Such a trend was noted in the 1940's, but it did not continue beyond the 1950's.[11] In recent years the evidence suggests that there is no difference in educational achievement between those black children who spend all their lives in northern inner-city urban schools and those who migrated from the south. However, there is still a North-South difference in average achievement scores of both black and white children.[12]

Psychological Explanations

Psychological explanations stress factors such as individual motivation, self-image, delay of gratification, anxiety, achievement expectancy, and the like. Those who emphasize these positions assert that lower-status children are low in achievement motivation,[13] have unrealistically high aspiration levels,[14] have incomplete or inadequate self-imges,[15] have negative self-images and a preference for things white,[16] have an inability to delay gratification,[17] and are frustrated when required to learn or held to high educational standards.[18] It is also contended that academic aspirations are depressed by the effects of discrimination on previous and present generations and that these children and their families perceive no economic or social rewards which they could realistically hope to attain through academic achievement.[19] Students with these social-psychological handicaps, combined with low motivation, are expected to be inattentive, hyperactive, hostile, and aggressive. While such explanations assert that academic retardation is a consequence of these motivational and behavioral handicaps, it is also conceivable that the handicaps are a consequence of educational deprivation and social rejection. Regardless of the explanation, when one finds a disproportionate number of psychologically impaired children in a school system, one cannot realistically deal with this problem in terms of individual clinical methods and therapy. Instead, one must address the problem of bringing about the necessary changes within the educational system which itself produces such casualties.

Sociological-Cultural Explanations

The last explanatory category to be discussed, the sociological-cultural, emphasizes cultural, class, and environmental differences as determining factors in the low academic achievement of minority group students. Such environmental conditions place limitations on the student's ability to profit from formal educational experiences. Some specific environmental features cited as inhibiting learning are neighborhood crime and delinquency,[20] broken homes,[21] the kind of poverty that sends children to school without breakfast and without adequate rest and that prevents parents from providing quiet places of study.[22] Other factors cited include overcrowded living quarters, deteriorated and unsanitary housing, no books in the home, and the strong influence of peers among lower-status children, conditions interpreted as adversely affecting the desire to pursue academic learning.[23] The linguistic patterns of lower-status students, particularly black children, also are said to inhibit academic learning.[24] Considerable evidence has been found to demonstrate that blacks have developed structurally differentiated dialectal variants of English and other European languages, indicating ethnic distinctiveness in areas of expressive culture.[25] The difficulty turns on the point that the school curriculum is based on "standard English," which presumably presents the black child with a Promethean barrier to academic mastery. This position appears to require a separation of black subculture and mainstream culture. An alternative position could be developed based on a biculturation assumption, however. It should be noted that the data cited show a consistent relationship between social and cultural status and academic achievement, and on this basis a causal relationship is often assumed to exist. But it is critical to note that no causal relationship has been demonstrated.

If sociological explanations are accepted, then the most direct way to increase academic achievement of students who are victims of their conditions is to change those conditions, an approach that would necessitate a vast program of social change. However, there is evidence that the academic achievement of socially devalued children can be improved without changes in the pattern of sociological deprivation, given improved quality of education.[26] The position taken by the sociocultural explanation should be approached cautiously because it provides an all too easy cop-out. Since improved education would have to await massive changes in other societal features, it is a formula for maintaining the status quo in the schools. Witness the Nixon administration's approach to the interrelated problems of de facto segregation of schools and segregated housing patterns in the North. Furthermore, as Clark indicates, those in control of the public schools do not have significant decision-making power within the larger society. The only process over which they have effective control is education; thus, it is in that domain that they must exercise their power to improve the quality of education. Besides, only when educational quality is held constant will the influence of other factors on learning be ascertainable.

In assessing current endeavors to educate minority children, Edmund Gordon and D. A. Wilkerson made the following statement:

Most of what is being done in the area of curriculum change is being done in a tradition of unscientific innovation. . . . Many of the innovations consume considerable time and money. Few of them are based on identifiable premises or viable hypotheses. Very often these innovations appear to have resulted from isolated, poorly controlled trial and error discoveries. . . . For example, there is little evidence or theoretical basis for judging either homogeneous or heterogeneous groupings as providing the more effective learning situation. Homogeneous grouping may, indeed, provide an easier teaching situation, but in practice it often serves simply to segregate the minority group children from their more privileged peers. Given the evidence suggesting that segregation is, per se, a handicap to the achievement of educational quality, and given, in addition, the school problem of the time, it might be well for school systems to examine the premise on which they have overwhelmingly adopted homogeneous grouping. It

is quite possible that the more difficult teaching situation provided by heterogeneous grouping is also the more productive in the total development of the
child.[27]

Gordon and Wilkerson make a similar criticism of certain structural changes in the programs, such as team teaching, utilization of
technology, modifications in teacher-pupil ratio, and the like. Assum-
ing the foregoing to be a valid analysis, the greatest contribution
behavioral science can make to the educational process, as it applies
to these children, would seem to be twofold: providing the necessary
theoretical and empirical basis for program development, and bringing the theoretical and methodological frameworks of behavioral
science to bear on the theoretical and applied problems of education.
More specifically, I am convinced that the fundamental contribution
the behavioral and social sciences can make to the process of edu-
cating lower-status children would be identification of patterns of
interrelatedness among individual learner characteristics, characteristics of the individual's social context, and outcomes in the teaching-
learning process. This position rests on the assumption that explanations based on dimensions or variables in a single domain cannot
account for the current level of academic performance of oppressed
children, as a group; nor can they provide a basis for remedy.

Inadequacy of Theory and Research in the Behavioral Sciences

If the foregoing is valid, then the question becomes what does
behavioral science have in the way of theoretical frameworks, methods, and empirical findings that reflect this interactive point of view?
In reviewing the literature one is struck by the extent to which
lower-status minority children, particularly black children, are separated from families, and the further separation of black children and
black families from the black community. But the most glaring factor concerns the separation of the black community from the surrounding white community. It seems obvious that we who are concerned about black children must think about them in relation to
black families and the black community, never forgetting that this
entire configuration is embedded in a society which devalues everything black.

A second realization, which had a great impact on me, concerns
the essentially negative nature of the research findings and interpreta-

tions. If the black child feels disdain or hatred for his group, and, therefore, for himself, and experiences himself as incomplete, then one would expect such factors to have negative effects on his behavior and experience.

The "Negro" family is portrayed as having a deviant life style, a style distinct from all other segments of the society. More often than not the father has deserted the family; the mother, frustrated because of her own unfulfilled needs and wishes, reacts harshly and rejects the children. Her frustration generally is a "causal" factor in her having more "illegitimate" children. The children, in turn, react to this hostile atmosphere by becoming aggressive, nontrusting, and uneducable. They experience unusual difficulty in differentiating between male and female roles, and cross-role adoptions are the rule. By the time he is three or four years old, the black child is aware of racial differences including a knowledge of the usual associated stereotypes, but he is slow to make racial distinctions. His parents (mother) are not able to help him with questions and anxiety concerning black-white issues and concerns. He frequently chooses white dolls and white friends and often identifies himself as white or shows a pained reluctance to "admit" he is "Negro." While much of the direct manifestation of "self-hate" disappears by the time the child is seven or eight years of age, definite indications of it exist even later; for example, "shooting" dope to escape the image, or "pimping" and having illegitimate children to deny it.[28]

Thus, the attention given so far to characteristics of lower-status children has given rise to sweeping generalizations, many of them highly questionable. The tendency is to identify certain conditions and characteristics found frequently in some lower-status children and then to assume these factors to be typical of the group. As indicated earlier, concurrence between certain conditions or characteristics and low academic achievement is given a causal interpretation. These theories can be questioned on the grounds of their failure to account for the full spectrum of findings in the various empirical studies. For example, what about that 33 percent to 77 percent in the Clark studies,[29] or the 87 percent in the Greenwald and Oppenheim study,[30] and the 46 percent to 68 percent in Morland's[31] studies who did not select white dolls as being "like themselves?" How does one account for Boyd's findings of a higher aspiration level in blacks compared to whites when groups were matched for age, IQ, and socioeconomic status?[32] The Lotts' study suggests that blacks can have high and realistic levels of occupational aspirations.[33] It is of interest to note that, when empirical results are in the unexpected direction, usually they are interpreted to be consistent with theoretical expectations. The concept of "unrealistic (high) aspiration level" seems to serve that purpose. Since the validity of a theory or conceptual system rests upon its ability to explain and predict, in these instances one has to wonder about theory-conserving operations. The history of this country is replete with instances of the creation of theories to demonstrate the inferiority of blacks; theories that can provide justification for the oppression of blacks; self-serving theories directed to maintaining the oppressor's illusions of his own innate superiority.[34] Historically, biological or genetic factors have been invoked as explanatory modes to account for the status of blacks; today the vogue is to call forth environmental factors as explanatory modes. However, it is of small benefit to blacks whether an environmental hypothesis is chosen over a genetic one, if the explanation remains at the level of the black individual or family and does not begin to deal with forces in the larger society. Contemporary social deprivation theories may be viewed as substituting environmental unchangeability for biologically determined immutability. Also, as stated earlier, most of the theoretical explanations for low academic achievement cited tend to locate its causes within the child and his family. Now, manifestly, it is logical to have the remedy, designed for intervention into a condition, rest upon one's concept of its causes. Thus, if the causes of academic failure among lower-status children are deemed to be within the child or his family, then this will be the point of focus for change. If it is thought to also reside within the social context of the child and family, that domain will be emphasized as well. The basic orientation implicitly or explicitly adopted by the social scientist will move him in one direction or another in theory and research.

If the behavioral and social sciences are to realize their full potential in terms of the contributions they can make to the education of black and other oppressed minority children, they must modify theory and the research flowing therefrom so that the child and his family are not viewed in isolation from their social contexts. This means a modification of perspective.

Another critical feature of the theoretical positions and empirical studies cited concerns the failure to view the black community as the highly complex, structured system that it is. The black writer Ralph Ellison placed this issue in perspective when asked by a group of young black writers to comment on how they might more accurately portray the complexity of the human condition, using the black experience as a theme. Ellison, among other things, stated that the black writer would never see his subjects so long as he accepted the black family as a broken one and a matriarchy, or Harlem as "piss on the wall and blood on the stairs. Such stereotypes, as all stereotypes, have some grain of truth in them, but they do not come close to reflecting the complexity of the black condition. . . ."[35] In the face of this it is interesting to note that the concentration of the literature is on the lowest income, most oppressed black families and individuals. The findings from this group are used as an index to "understanding" and "explaining and describing" blacks. Obviously, to utilize information from this narrow spectrum of the black population as a basis for describing, explaining, and predicting for blacks creates conditions for gross error. This practice probably explains some of the contradictions and paradoxes in the literature regarding blacks. Social and behavioral scientists must be aware of the protoassumptions of the theoretical positions and research methodologies with which they approach the study of blacks generally if these fields are to yield their full potential with respect to this segment of the population.

The perspective advanced here emphasizes the interdependence of the black child and family with other levels of society, and emphasizes the recognition of the black community as a complex social system. Further, this perspective shifts the focus from the behaviors of individuals to recurrent interchanges between people, that is, to the context in which social behavior takes place.

If the analysis advanced here has any validity, it raises implications for social and behavioral science, in terms of the need to subject theories, concepts, and methodologies, as applied to oppressed minority groups, to careful scrutiny with a view toward assessing how they operate when black people are the object of their focus. The significance of this assertion seems obvious when one reflects on the nature and function of theories, concepts, and so forth. Theories have their origin in the need to understand, explain, or predict phenomena, an activity each of us engages in daily, implicitly or explicitly. Theories or their concepts may be ordered along the following continuums: implicit-explicit, specificity-generality, concreteness-abstractness. Those of physics are characterized by explicitness, generality, and abstractness. Those of the behavioral and social sciences are somewhere between the polar points of the continuums, having been developed within the Western-Anglo-European heritage in order to explain and understand the behavior of those from that same heritage. It is legitimate to inquire whether these constructions, as they stand, give rise to valid explanations when applied to those who do not fully share that heritage. We know that, ostensibly, the same behavior arising in different contexts may have different antecedents and consequences. The obvious case involves similar behaviors arising in different cultures.

H. C. Kelman has produced a cogent analysis of the role of social values in the development of science.[36] It is his contention that values (I would add perspectives) not only determine the directions scientific activity takes at any given time, but they also influence methodological considerations. Values direct the choice of theories or models, direct focus, whether on strengths or weaknesses, and influence the nature of definitions of behavioral events. Definitions of events by members of the privileged majority often are negative in connotation as applied to blacks, and other oppressed minority groups. White analyzes several concepts in cognitive and dynamic schools of psychology such as "disadvantagement," "broken family," noting underlying assumptions of deficiency or abnormality or pathology.[37] He concludes that the cultural values of the dominant society are built into the definitions and carry adverse implications for blacks. It seems obvious that definitions of what is "normal," "healthy," "deviant," "pathologic," must relate to the conditions of a group's existence, to its interests, and to what it conceives as socially desirable and socially undesirable. Total acceptance and application of white definitions of "health," "pathology," "growth," "delay of gratification," among others, to blacks leads to the ironic situation Barbara Sizemore so ably formulates in her A/B conceptualization.[38] The paradigm is as follows: A creates a set of conditions for B. If B is to survive, he must respond in those ways having survival value. A defines this behavior as "sick" or "abnormal," but, in fact, B's response is natural and appropriate to the conditions. Any response which A would call normal would not have survival value for B. The plain facts are that blacks and whites do not live in the same social reality. That which is deviant behavior for a white might be healthy for a black and vice versa. Rosa Parks' refusal to sit in the "proper place" on that bus in Montgomery in 1955 was problem or deviant behavior from the vantage point of whites in the south. How would you define the behavior of a bright thirteen year old living in one of the more dehumanizing housing projects in Chicago, who almost daily had the choice of fighting or running, but who chose to fight? This child was referred to me with the complaint of being overly aggressive and hypersensitive to provocation. Clearly the healthy response in this situation was not running if we are concerned about the youngster's self-esteem, and psychological survival. The critical issue here concerns the perspective from which behavioral events are defined. For example, certain behaviors of black youth have been defined from the dominant culture view or perspective as "apathy or lack of communication with the school." This same behavior might well be defined from the black perspective as "failure of school officials (decision makers) to provide the black community with needed educational concepts, strategies, and tactics for successfully coping with a hostile white environment"; or majority designated "low achievement pressure or lack of information about the relevance of early stimulation" as "unequal distribution of valuable societal resources resulting from the use of race as an organizing principle of society"; or "pessimism about opportunities" as "the existence of racism in America and its legitimation by social and behavioral scientists who study the effects rather than the cause of genocide."

In addition to the formal definition of terms and selection of variables, there is also the issue of the operational definition of variables, an example being "deferred gratification" and its attendant "time orientation," where the lesser of two values chosen "now" over the greater one promised "tomorrow," is designated "inability to delay" and as indicative of a "present-time" orientation (negative). This is contrasted to behavior of the middle-class individual who chooses the object of greater value and is, thus, said to have "delay capacity" and a "future-time" orientation (positive). The writer could build an argument for insight into social reality on the part of the former. The difference between the two lies not so much in their different orientations to future time or, more specifically, to their actual futures. The future orientation of the middle-class person presumes, among other things, that an adequate supply of resources will be invested in the future, and that the future will be sufficiently stable to justify his investment, to permit utilization or consumption of his investment at a time, place, and manner of his own choosing, and to make possible greater satisfaction. It is precisely the lower-status child's awareness of the future that moves him in the direction of "a bird in the hand." It is instructive in this regard to observe the behavior of investors on Wall Street when events occur to produce uncertainties in the future. At such times their selling and buying behaviors have all the earmarks of "inability to delay."[39] In other words, social and behavioral scientists must examine carefully their operational definitions and must ask themselves if the same set of operations-defining concepts, such as "female dependence," "unresolved oedipal conflict," and "deferred gratification" can be applied with equal effectiveness to varying segments of the society, particularly to those whose conditions differ markedly from those of mainstream America.

I submit that the objections raised throughout the discussion point to factors that militate against behavioral and social sciences making the maximum contribution to the education of black and other oppressed minority children. The question, then, becomes: Are there alternatives to the present order? My response is a confident "yes."

The Systems Approach: An Alternative to the Mental Health Model

The perspective advanced in this discussion, with its emphasis on the interdependence of child and family with other levels of society, the heterogeneity of blacks (and other oppressed groups), the recognition of the black community as a complex social system, the shift of focus from behaviors of individuals to recurrent interchanges between people, is an alternative that may properly be called a social systems approach. It addresses many of the objections raised to the current modal approach, which reflects its white, Anglo perspective.

The system conception as put forth here has been called by some an "aggregate" or "growth and development" model while those perspectives which focus on the individual or his family have been called "mental health," "treatment," or "pathology" models.[40] Fundamental conceptual distinctions characterize these two modes of approach. Spelling out some of these distinctions will facilitate our grasp of the assumptions underlying the various theoretical and methodological approaches.

The mental health model focuses on the individual in an attempt to understand or resolve a problem. There is an implicit assumption here that the individual is responsible for his condition. The aggregate or systems model is social-psychological, economic-political, and biological-cultural. This model is concerned with systems and subsystems, social and psychological, in interrelationship. In research, the point of focus is interchange between systems. As an approach it does not facilitate unidimensional explanation. For example, in attempting to understand the determinants of the present pattern of educational performance of low-status children, it would look for complex patterns of interrelatedness of class, cultural, social, and racial inequities, and their various effects upon the student, recognize that a change in context may be attended by a change in behavior, that is, a *change in the relationship patterns of the systems*. This approach possibly can begin to put some of the various findings regarding blacks into a coherent scheme with altered interpretations to take into consideration the environmental or social context of those studied.

For the mental health model, community tends to be defined as a political unit, a place from where the subjects come, or as a geographic unit. The aggregate model views the individual in relation to the community, defined as "system of systems" and views the community as in dynamic interrelationship with a larger system. The theories and concepts of such sociologists as Talcott Parsons;[41] and psychologists such as Kurt Lewin,[42] among others, provide the basis for a systems approach to thinking about man and his context.

From the point of view of the mental health model, when the individual alone is considered, the focus is on such intrapsychic factors such as id, ego, and superego. From the systems point of view the concepts utilized consider such aspects as system boundaries, open and closed systems, roles, statuses, structure, communication, communications barrier, intra- and intersystem relationships.[43] All of these variables can add to our understanding of the relations of individuals to their social contexts.

The mental health model focuses on pathology and deficiencies, while the systems model has the goal of exploring the conditions which impede or stimulate positive functioning or growth. To this end, the base, in research, is on "normal" growth processes and the social systems which influence them. The mental health focus insists that the line of causation runs from the individual to society. The systems approach recognizes the interaction between societal processes and individual behavior. For example, the weaknesses of individuals or families do not cause racism, that major pathology afflicting blacks and other racial-ethnic minorities.

For the mental health model, evaluation or assessment is program focused in terms of the explicit criteria to which the program is addressed. It does not recognize that any program has both intended and unintended outcomes. In the systems model the individual-in-relation-to-his-social-systems is studied for insights and understandings that may lead to social action as well as to information regarding the status of the program, with reference to the criteria it seeks to achieve.

In his treatment of General Systems Theory (GST), Ludwig Bertalanffy states that "general systems theory contends that there are principles of systems in general or in defined subclasses of systems irrespective of the nature of systems or their components, or of the relations of forces between them."[44] Thus, GST is general in that it attempts to examine all types of systems. A system is an organization of elements united in a form of regular interaction and interdependence. GST as an approach to organizing and looking at phenomena is thus applicable to the cell (biological system), to the individual (psychological system), to groups or society (social systems). The focus of the perspective offered is on psychological and social systems.

The concept of a social system has been treated comprehensively by Talcott Parsons and associates.[45] A social system is an aggregation of social roles or persons bound together by a pattern of mutual interaction and interdependence. It has boundaries that enable us to distinguish the internal from the external environment and, typically, it is a system for social units smaller than itself and a subsystem for social units larger than itself.

Billingsley depicts the black family as a social system embedded in a network of mutually interdependent relationships with the black community and wider society. Just as the family is a subsystem of the black community, so are various patterns of interactions (*dyads*: father-son; mother-daughter; brother-sister; *triads*: grandmother-mother-daughter, and so forth) subsystems of the family, which for them is a social system. The individuals in these various patterns, in turn, are subsystems to the larger interactive patterns, dyad, triad, and so forth, with the family.

A key consideration in all of this concerns the mutually interdependent relations existing between the family and its members, on the one hand, and the family and the black community, and the black community and wider society on the other hand.

The educational subsystem of the society is among those having an impact on the community and, through it, the family. It may be, among other things, that the nature of the relationship of the family to the community, and, in turn, the nature of the interchanges between school and community are key factors in the academic achievement of the child. It may be that, when the interchanges between the school and the child's community and family are mutually supportive, the school taking an initiating role in making itself a part of the child's community, academic achievement is positively affected. This perspective also conceives of blacks as a highly complex, heterogeneous, diverse people. Even though, in this country, black people are viewed as a group apart from other people, and as showing common intragroup attributes, behaviors, and conditions, great within-group variations are also obvious. Billingsley offers the concept "ethnic subsociety" as a means of capturing this duality.[46] This concept was taken from Milton Gordon's theoretical work.[47] An ethnic group is defined as a relatively large configuration of people with a "shared feeling of peoplehood." In this society such groups are organized around race, religion, national origin, or some combination of these. Gordon states that, common to the ethnic group,

is the social-psychological element of a special sense of both ancestral and future-oriented identification with the group. These are the "people" of my ancestors, therefore, they are my people, and will be the people of my children and their children. With members of other groups I may share political participation, occupational relationships, common civic enterprise, perhaps even an occasional warm friendship, but in a very special way, which history has decreed, I share a sense of indissoluble and intimate identity with this *group* and not *that* group within the larger society and the world.[48]

This conception seems to reflect the reality of the existence of black people. It also reflects the growing black consciousness or awareness of our peoplehood, which is evolving at a rapid rate in black communities throughout the country. While we are one, as members of a color-caste system and by virtue of our common peoplehood, we are not a homogeneous mass. Billingsley has depicted the black community as an ethnic subsociety.

Billingsley's conceptual model makes use of three dimensions in describing the black community as an ethnic subsociety. They are social dimensions on which members within an ethnic group vary, namely, social class, rural or urban residence, and region of the country lived in. For our purposes, then, black groups are not only blacks to be compared or contrasted with whites; they may also be upper class, middle class, or lower class, with northern, southern or western residence, with urban or rural backgrounds, and, significantly, they may be meaningfully compared and contrasted with each other. Consider the additional complexity added by further distinctions within an overall class level; for example, the lower class is divided into the nonworking poor, the working poor and the working nonpoor.

As indicated by Billingsley the significance of social class is not to be able to make such statements as middle-class whites and blacks have more in common than do middle- and lower-class blacks. Such a formulation obscures more than it reveals, and it fails to distinguish between the different types of identities people share. Gordon conceptualizes two types of identities people share: historical and participational identification.

> With a person of the same social class but of different ethnic group, one shares behavioral similarities but not a sense of peoplehood. With those of the same ethnic group but different social class, one shares the sense of peoplehood but not behavioral similarities. The only group which meets both these criteria are people of the same ethnic group and social class.[49]

As Billingsley suggests, even though social-class lines among blacks are less rigid than among other groups, social-class distinctions within the black community do provide a distinct basis of differentiation that helps to condition the lives of blacks. Hence, one would expect differential responses to external impingements, or interchanges with the various subsystems by people located at different positions in the structure, differential responses or interchanges that have implications for minority children's developmental status generally, and educational achievement in particular.

Summary and Conclusions

The perspective brought forth in this paper argues for new directions in the education of oppressed minority groups, and it addresses needed assessment of the theories, concepts, and methods of the social and behavioral sciences as applied to members of these groups, requisite to a fully meaningful contribution to innovative efforts in this area. A critical strategy necessary to break the familiar cycle involves an explicit recognition of the child's community, group, and culture. The learning environment must become a part of and be supportive of the child's community. This perspective considers the whole child, recognizes that he has both cognitive and affective needs, that he comes from a family, which exists as part of an ethnic subsociety, which is itself part of a larger society, which devalues the black child, family, and community, and recognizes that the process of education must address itself to these dimensions explicitly. Even where cognitive achievement does occur, it is not enough if such achievement is attained by denial of the validity of the child's own culture. Frantz Fanon's *Black Skin, White Masks* speaks eloquently to the pernicious effects of the education attained in the latter terms.[50] In effect, it leads to "gaining the brain but losing the soul." Thus, the social and behavioral sciences must address these issues if they are to be positive forces in the educational process as it acts upon these children. A central implication of this perspective is the necessity for a redefinition of educational programs. A change in definition would require a shift in focus in the evaluation process from the child (conceived of primarily as a cognitive subsystem) to the whole person-in-a-social-context, not as a fragmented being separated from his surrounding. Given this perspective, research on a particular problem area would not be concerned only with narrowly defined approaches such as the evaluation of cognitive change as a function of pupils being exposed to programs of compensatory education, but would take into account those wider experiences that influence growth, positively or negatively. There is also a necessity and this is critical, for behavioral science research, concerned with understanding and resolving social problems, to be more explicit about its underlying assumptions, values, and goals. Laboratory-based research may be able to remain at the level of "pure knowledge," but research into problems concerned with understanding and resolving social problems cannot. Thus, a developmental model appears to be the appropriate one for the behavioral sciences, as applied in this area. This model incorporates growth as its value base. Academic mastery may be offered as a significant aspect of growth. It must be realized that neither the behavioral scientist nor the researcher, as a person, nor the processes or products of research are entirely value-free. The observations of the social scientist cannot be carried out from a wholly external vantage point; nor can the findings of social research stand by themselves as scientifically valid facts about the world. Further, the role of the social scientist cannot be totally separated from that of human being, of citizen, and of participant in social action. Further definition of the problem cannot be totally separated from those defining the problem. The selection of dimensions and measurement operations reflects the cultural and value perspective of those developing the concepts, defining dimensions, specifying operations, and so forth.

Finally, the social scientist is confronted with the question of the nature of the social forces his research represents or his theories reflect. What is the nature of the social processes they help to foster? What is the quality of the social values they help to promote? Rather than hiding behind "scientific objectivity," social and behavioral scientists are called upon to assume their responsibilities for the human beings in our society and become monitors of social justice. The foregoing represents some of the characteristics I would see in a humanistic behavioral science, as applied to the education of oppressed minority groups. These are the directions I think future developments in social and behavioral science must take if they are to *serve* all peoples of the society and not merely represent and protect the "White Anglo-Saxon Ideal."

Notes

1. Kenneth B. Clark, *A Possible Reality: A Design for the Attainment of High Academic Achievement for the Students of the Public Elementary and Junior High Schools of Washington, D. C.* (New York: Metropolitan Applied Research Center, Inc., 1970); E. W. Gordon and D. A. Wilkerson, *Compensatory Education for the Disadvantaged: Programs and Practices Preschool through College* (New York: College Entrance Examination Board, 1966).

2. Kenneth M. Stampp, *The Peculiar Institution—Slavery in the Ante-Bellum South* (New York: Vantage Books, 1956).

3. A. R. Jensen, "How Much Can We Boost IQ and Scholastic Achievement?" *Harvard Educational Review* 39 (Winter 1969), 1-123.

4. C. A. Valentine, "Deficit, Difference and Bicultural Models of Afro-American Behavior," *Harvard Educational Review* 41 (May 1971), 137-57.

5. Clark, *op. cit.*

6. Hilda Knoblock and Benjamin Pasamanick, "Environmental Factors Affecting Human Development before and after Birth," *Pediatrics* 26 (1960), 210-18.

7. S. A. Kirk, *Early Education of the Mentally Retarded* (Urbana: University of Illinois Press, 1958).

8. J. S. Coleman *et al.*, *Equality of Educational Opportunity* (Washington, D. C.: Government Printing Office, 1966).

9. Otto Klineberg, *Negro Intelligence and Selective Migration* (New York: Columbia University, 1935).

10. T. Pettigrew, *A Profile of the Negro American* (Princeton, New Jersey: Van Nostrand, 1964).

11. Clark, *op. cit.*

12. Coleman *et al.*, *op. cit.*

13. B. C. Rosen, "Race, Ethnicity and the Achievement Syndrome," *American Sociological Review* 24 (February 1959), 47-60; P. H. Mussen, "Differences between the TAT Responses of Negro and White Boys," *Journal of Consulting Psychology* 17 (October 1953), 373-76; Martin Deutsch, "The Disadvantaged Child and the Learning Process," in A. Harry Passow (ed.), *Education in Depressed Areas* (New York: Bureau of Publications, Teachers College, Columbia University, 1963).

14. D. Ausubel and P. Ausubel, "Ego Development among Segregated Negro Children," in Passow, *op. cit.*

15. Lee Rainwater, "Crucible of Identity: The Negro Lower-Class Family," in T. Parsons and K. B. Clark (eds.), *The Negro American* (Boston: Beacon Press, 1967), 160-204.

16. H. Proshansky and P. Newton, "The Nature and Meaning of Negro Self-Identity," in M. Deutsch, I. Katz, and A. Jensen (eds.), *Social Class, Race, and Psychological Development* (New York: Holt, Rinehart, and Winston, Inc., 1967).

17. Walter Mischel, "Father-Absence and Delay of Gratification: Cross-Cultural Comparisons," *Journal of Abnormal and Social Psychology* 63 (No. 1, 1961), 116-24.

18. Proshansky and Newton, *op. cit.*

19. *Ibid.*

20. W. B. Miller, "Low Class Culture as a Generating Milieu of Gang Delinquency," *Journal of Social Issues* 14 (No. 1, 1958), 5-19.

21. Mischel, *op. cit.*

22. Deutsch, *op. cit.*

23. Clark, *op. cit.*

24. D. P. Ausubel, "How Reversible are the Cognitive and Motivational

Effects of Cultural Deprivation? Implications for teaching the Culturally Deprived Child," *Urban Education* 1 (Summer 1964), 16-38; M. Whiteman and M. Deutsch, "Social Disadvantage as Related to Intelligence and Language Development," in Deutsch, Katz, and Jensen (eds.), *op. cit.*

25. T. Kochman, "Toward an Ethnography of Black American Speech," in N. Whitten and J. Szwed, *Afro-American Anthropology: Contemporary Perspectives* (New York: Free Press, 1970); W. Stewart, "Urban Negro Speech: Sociolinguistic Factors Affecting English Teaching," in R. W. Shuy (ed.), *Social Dialects and Language Learning* (Champaign, Illinois: National Council of Teachers of English, 1965).

26. Kirk, *op. cit.*

27. Gordon and Wilkerson, *op. cit.*, 169.

28. Rainwater, *op. cit.*

29. K. B. Clark and Mamie Clark, "Racial Identification and Preferences in Negro Children," in T. M. Newcomb and E. I. Hartley (eds.), *Readings in Social Psychology* (New York: Holt, 1947).

30. H. J. Greenwald and D. B. Oppenheim, "Reported Magnitude of Self-Misidentification among Negro Children—Artifact?" *Journal of Personality and Social Psychology* 8 (January 1968), 49-52.

31. J. K. Morland, "Racial Acceptance and Preference of Nursery School Children in a Southern City," *Merrill-Palmer Quarterly* 8 (October 1962), 271-80.

32. G. F. Boyd, "The Levels of Aspiration of White and Negro Children in a Non-Segregated Elementary School," *Journal of Social Psychology* 36 (November 1952), 191-96.

33. A. J. Lott and B. Lott, *Negro and White Youth: A Psychological Study in a Border State* (New York: Holt, Rinehart and Winston, 1963).

34. Stampp, *op. cit.*

35. Ralph Ellison, "A Very Stern Discipline," *Harper's Magazine* (March 1967), 87.

36. H. C. Kelman, *A Time to Speak: On Human Values and Social Research* (San Francisco: Jossey-Bass, Inc., 1968).

37. J. L. White, "Guidelines for Black Psychologists," *Black Scholar* 1 (March 1970), 52-57.

38. B. Sizemore, "Separatism: A Reality Approach to Inclusion?" in R. L. Green (ed.), *Racial Crisis in American Education* (Chicago: Follett Educational Corp., 1969).

39. E. Liebow, *Talley's Corner* (Boston: Little, Brown, 1967).

40. D. Adelson, "A Concept of Comprehensive Community Mental Health," in D. Adelson and B. C. Kalis (eds.), *Community Psychology and Mental Health: Perspectives and Challenges* (Scranton, Pennsylvania: Chandler Publishing Company, 1970).

41. Talcott Parsons, *The Social System* (New York: Free Press, 1951).

42. Kurt Lewin, *Resolving Social Conflicts* (New York: Harper, 1948).

43. L. Von Bertalanffy, "General Systems Theory and Psychiatry," in S. Arieti (ed.), *American Handbook of Psychiatry*, Vol. III (New York: Basic

Books, 1966); D. Cartwright and A. Zander (eds.), *Group Dynamics: Research and Theory* (Evanston, Illinois: Row, Peterson, 1960).

44. *Ibid.,* 708.

45. Parsons, *op. cit.*; T. Parsons and R. Bales, *Family Socialization and Interaction Process* (New York: Free Press, 1955).

46. Andrew Billingsley, *Black Families in White America* (Englewood Cliffs, New Jersey: Prentice-Hall, 1968).

47. M. Gordon, *Assimilation in American Life* (New York: Oxford University Press, 1964).

48. *Ibid.,* 29.

49. *Ibid.,* 53.

50. Frantz Fanon, *Black Skins, White Masks* (New York: Grove Press, 1967).

7. Alienation of Afro-American Children

Curriculum and Evaluation
in American Schools

Diana T. Slaughter

The thesis of this paper is that school curricula and evaluation of those curricula contribute to the progressive alienation of Afro-American school children. There are discrepancies between the expressed institutional goals of the school and its normative practices with regard to the human needs of developing black children. The perception of these discrepancies by the children adversely affects both their attitudes toward the school and their conceptions of their relationship to it. Because these children are alienated by the school experience, many do not choose to learn. The children's academic retardation is reflected in achievement test data, the reports of school personnel, high truancy and dropout rates, and similar manifestations of discomfort and dissatisfaction with the school experience. The implications for educational and research alternatives are clear: if many such children fail in school because they do not *want* to learn there, then some effort must be made to determine how the children perceive the school experience, as well as how the school experience influences the children's self-perceptions.

This paper was originally prepared for the Social Science Research Council Subcommittee on Learning and the Education Process: Work Group on Self-Concept, 1971.

Critique of Compensatory Education: The Complexity of the Child's Educational Experience

Achievement test results from urban public schools attended by a majority of Afro-American children reveal a progressive decline in academic performance, relative to national norms, with each additional year in school. First dramatically portrayed in the unpublished HARYOU report,[1] and discussed by Clark in *Dark Ghetto*,[2] the pattern of decline, beginning most noticeably in third grade, has since been publicly reported by several city school systems, and it was substantiated in at least one research effort of my own.[3] While the data are primarily cross-sectional, the findings have been consistent enough to suggest longitudinal implications. Longitudinal data collected by Roberts[4] and Slaughter[5] provide additional support for this view. Roberts reported a decline in I.Q. for the same group of children due to an increase in chronological age (CA) while mental age (MA) remained constant. Slaughter found that over a five-year period, from kindergarten through fourth grade, the percentage of the same group of children scoring at or above national norms on achievement tests declined sharply. Compensatory education, partially developed in response to these and similar findings, has had a corresponding emphasis upon the socialization of those behaviors presumed related to school readiness and the acquisition of cognitive skills.[6]

Compensatory educational programs have not proved responsive to the demand for successful and meaningful education of large numbers of these children, particularly in regard to stimulation and maintenance of higher levels of cognitive development, as reflected in standard performance criteria.[7] Programs for cognitive enrichment, remedial reading, ungraded classrooms, team teaching, and parental involvement have hardly dented the bureaucracy of the educational system. The effectiveness of any planned educational program is usually dependent upon the ethos of the school community in which it is introduced.[8] Specific innovations such as programmed learning have limited benefits. Teachers frequently are freed from teaching rote or associative learning tasks, but the more fundamental issues of children's concept formation and positive personality development cannot be so addressed.[9]

Consultantship services also have limited impact. The consultant is frequently not an integral part of the school community, and thus cannot evaluate his own effectiveness from an educational perspective. Effectiveness with a few of the school personnel is often vitiated by the school's high rate of staff turnover. Conversely, focus on individual children has often had limited benefit for both consultant and child. Typically, at the conclusion of the academic year the child enters a new classroom with a new teacher. The diversity of teaching methods used and the new teacher's inattention to the child's educational history often combine to negate any earlier gains.[10]

In most compensatory educational programs therefore, the problem of effecting permanent change is crucial at all levels of the educational experience. Limited permanent change in children's performances most probably results when there is deemphasis on the school as a social institution, and overemphasis on the children's personal characteristics, in contrast to the relationship between their human needs and the social milieu of the school.

Innovators of compensatory educational programs typically conceive of curricula narrowly in terms of textbook materials and supplementary educational aids. Programs are limited to the school building and the sequence of events during the days and months of the school year. Small wonder that there is little permanent behavioral or attitudinal change among the inhabitants of that building. Our experiences and those of other behavioral scientists would suggest that the school is a complex social institution involving the community in which the school building resides; the school children; the respective parents; teachers and the educational and personal histories they bring; and administrators and their personal and professional liaisons, which range from current professional affiliations to perceived sources of occupational mobility within the educational system. The educational experience of the child is a function of the interaction of all segments of the social system of the school and the contribution of their respective curricula.[11]

The curriculum of a school is best defined in terms of the school's institutional goals and not its educational materials or facilities. Miller's definition, for example, is useful: "curriculum is treated as the instructional objectives of the school, the ways in which these outcomes are allocated in specific sequences, and learning materials provided to aid in their achievement."[12] This definition has particular significance if all sectors of the school social system are considered. The institutional goals of the school, for example, may be perceived differently by students, parents, teachers, and administrators. Broadly speaking, however, at least two classes of institutional goals may be identified: rationalist and developmental,[13] or traditional and modern.[14]

Behavioral outcomes, particularly in terms of intellectual performance criteria, are emphasized in the traditional schools. At its extreme, the curriculum is composed of a relatively fixed body of knowledge to be passed to successive generations. A coherent consistent set of assumptions and implicit value systems characterizes this curriculum. Arendt is perhaps one of its most sophisticated advocates:

Insofar as the child is not yet acquainted with the world, he must be gradually introduced to it . . . the educators here stand in relation to the young as representatives of a world for which they must assume responsibility although they themselves did not make it . . . the teacher's qualification consists in knowing the world and being able to instruct others about it, but his authority rests on his assumption of responsibility for that world. Vis-à-vis the child it is as though he were a representative of all adult inhabitants, pointing out the details and saying to the child: this is our world . . . the function of the school is to teach children what the world is like and not to instruct them in the art of living. Since the world is old . . . learning inevitably turns toward the past, no matter how much living will spend itself in the present . . . the line drawn between children and adults should signify that one can neither educate adults nor treat children as though they were grown up . . . Education is the point at which we decide whether we love the world enough to assume responsibility for it and by the same token save it from that ruin which, except for renewal, except for the coming of the new and young, would be inevitable. And education, too, is where we decide whether we love our children enough not to expel them from our world and leave them to their own devices . . . but to prepare them in advance for the task of renewing a common world.[15]

The broad institutional goals of the traditional school, so eloquently stated by Arendt, however, are not reflected in the "traditional" schools which the majority of Afro-American children attend. Arendt argues that emphasis on child individuation and the merits of the communal life of childhood thwarts the achievement of education in the traditional sense. From our perspective, the emphasis on child individuation also does not characterize schools attended by the majority of black children.

The developmental or modern view of education has found recent

support in current emphases upon ego psychology and the significance of such concepts as "autonomous ego functions" and "competence motivation."[16] These concepts suggest that educational goals
ought to incorporate the totality of the child's growth and development. Behavioral scientists have often stated that education must
take cognizance of the principles of child development in planning
curriculum;[17] that teacher attitudes influence classroom climate and,
hence, the contextual experience in which children learn;[18] that
pupil characteristics, including social and cultural background, are
important variables in the educational experience.[19] These and many
more such findings are frequently ignored in the programmatic efforts of adults who want to affect the educational experiences of
school children.

According to the developmental view, the child's personal-social
and cognitive development is characterized by increasing differentiation, specialization, and integration of each of his innate behavioral
systems. The explicit goal of quality education is the stimulation of
this development, primarily through the kind of instruction and
training provided, and particularly as preparatory to adult life in a
modern bureaucratic and technological society.[20]

The behavioral sciences, therefore, do provide some guidelines for
quality education for children. They should, as a group, continue to
perform up to their maximum capacity on standard intelligence and
achievement tests; be viewed by educators as performing up to grade-
level expectations in every classroom; demonstrate impulse control
within the limits of age-range expectations; demonstrate those qualities which Biber[21] refers to as a capacity for sensitivity to the world
around them, for interest in exploration and discovery learning, for
continued growth in cognitive power and intellectual mastery, for
growth in healthy autonomous functioning, and for divergent thinking. What is most important, perhaps, is that children should, as a
group, demonstrate self-understanding and self-respect.

Despite their differences, the traditional and developmental views
both emphasize the personal characteristics of the child which are to
be influenced by education. Although both views, when well represented, acknowledge the complexity of the educational experience
for any child, neither is reflected in the educational experience of
many black children because neither perspective, as practiced, considers the relationship between human needs of Afro-American chil-

dren and the expressed institutional goal of the school: quality education, whatever the theoretical orientation.

Extensive data which indicate an absence of observable signs of quality education in urban ghetto schools now exist.[22] Such "signs" may range from adequate physical facilities to an adequately trained teaching staff. Some have suggested that the absence of these signs does not necessarily imply an absence of quality education,[23] while others have stated that whatever the immediate aims of education, academic performance criteria have little long-term predictive value for adult success,[24] and even formal education may be irrelevant as a solution to the problems of societal inequities.[25] Still others have suggested that the failure to educate black American children is but part of the failure to educate all American children.[26]

Educational outcomes, as measured by performance criteria, may be of limited long-term significance if intelligence and achievement are viewed as spontaneous operant adaptations[27] resulting from the interaction of the child and his environment[28] and not as habitual respondent fixations to predetermined stimuli. While these outcomes may not be indicative of the innate biological inferiority of black Americans, they cannot be disregarded. Many educators themselves have concurred in the belief that, even when curriculum and evaluation seem to be similar, differences in educational outcomes still emerge.[29] We believe the outcomes reflect the impact of cultural discontinuities between the pseudoassimilationist stance of curriculum and evaluation strategies used with black American children in schools, and the limited attention to their sociocultural and historical realities in pursuit of these strategies. The absence of quality education for Afro-American children reflected in their limited acquisition of academic skills must also be viewed as a contributory factor in their progressive dehumanization by the school as a social institution. We are especially concerned about the effects of value discontinuities between black American communities and the schools, and distinctions between normative practices relative to black children even when values are congruent, for the integration of the black child's multiple self-perceptions, his self-respect and self-acceptance.

We must consider the possibility that schools which service black American children do not view themselves as social institutions responsible for meeting human needs, thereby providing an education congruent with the social experiences and aspirations of Afro-Americans. If the school as a social institution does not meet its *raison d'être,* it will inevitably produce a sense of estrangement in the children it services. We appropriately turn to a discussion of *alienation,* a self-referent concept that emphasizes the relationship between the social order and the individual as perceived by the individual.

Alienation: The Individual Self-Concept and the Social Order

Schacht has recently completed an important review of the historical roots and usages of alienation in an effort to clarify its meaning. He reports that it typically has had at least two general usages: (1) the disparity between the individual's actual condition and his essential nature (Alienation I), and (2) the voluntary separation from the individual of something importantly his (Alienation II). Alienation I is most familiar. It could refer to the separation of modern man from meaning in life achieved through the positive experiences of work, intimate relations, and personal self-knowledge and self-acceptance. Alienation II, according to Schacht, is not always undesirable, however. Voluntary delegation of individual particularity and will as perceived by Hegel can be for the social good if the *social substance* (sociocultural institutions) reflects the social creations of man while acting in his essential nature as a human being. Individual particularity is surrendered for the purpose of achieving universality or a sense of unity with mankind, that is, for achieving a renewed sense of self. Alienation II is the result of an individual's deliberate effort to overcome the discordant relationship between *his* particular self, and *the* essential self. Schacht evaluates Hegel:

It may be that Hegel's conception of man's essential nature is not completely satisfactory. But there is much to be said for his basic point: that the most important thing about man is his capacity for spiritual life; and that spiritual life in its completeness involves both distinct individuality and participation in a social, cultural, and political community. Support for this suggestion is to be found in the fact that most people would not consider life to be truly *human* if either of these elements were completely lacking.[30]

For Marx, of course, the essence of the social substance is the political economy, and the product of the individual's labor is in fact the objectification of his individual will and personality. The complete surrender of one's product, or control of its manifestation and distribution, is alienating, whether or not the individual is conscious of it. Both the Marxist and Hegelian views of alienation are important. The Marxist view appears to emphasize the adverse consequences of surrendering all that has been produced by an essential self, and the Hegelian view emphasizes that sociocultural institutions are created by man in his image, the boldest assertion of his humanity.

Alienations I and II both have direct relevance for discussions of quality education for Afro-American children. Alienation I occurs when the curriculum and evaluation strategies of public schools require Afro-American children to suppress their understanding of the value and normative differences in their immediate families and communities which they bring to the middle-class-value-oriented school; it occurs when children perceive that their parents in these communities are denied or excluded from decision-making power in the school social system—the family cannot assume its protective function for the child. Alienation II occurs when the schools do not transmit information as to the history, traditions, and folkways of the broader Afro-American communities, and when the achievements and competencies of black Americans are ignored or negated. These objective events produce the subjective sense of alienation—the felt sense of estrangement with which black children and their parents must cope if they are to make the process of education a meaningful and viable enterprise for them. This dilemma is posed whether or not the school is rationalist or developmental in orientation; adequate or inadequate in administration; relevant or irrelevant for future adult success or the problems of societal inequities.

Some sociologists have had a particular interest in social institutions, and in the relationship of the individual self to institutional goals (values) and normative practices. Merton, for example, discusses the relationship between social structure and *anomie*[31] in two essays where his primary aim is:

to discover how some social structures exert a definite pressure upon certain persons in the society to engage in nonconforming rather than conforming conduct. If we can locate groups peculiarly subject to such pressures, we should expect to find fairly high rates of deviant behavior in these groups, not because the human beings comprising them are compounded of distinctive biological tendencies, but because they are responding normally to the social situation in which they find themselves.[32]

Merton outlines several possible types of interactions between culturally valued goals on the one hand and institutional normative
practices on the other and describes their relevance for personal
styles of adaptation. He believes deviant behavior is encouraged by a
social system as a consequence of perceived discrepancies which the
system itself stimulates between cultural values and institutional
practices among its members:

> Of those located in the lower reaches of the social structure, the culture makes
> incompatible demands. On the one hand, they are asked to orient their conduct
> toward the prospect of large wealth . . . and on the other they are denied effec-
> tive opportunities to do so institutionally. The consequence of this structural
> inconsistency is a high rate of deviant behavior . . . A high frequency of deviant
> behavior is not generated merely by lack of opportunity or by this exaggerated
> pecuniary emphasis. A comparatively rigidified class structure, a caste order,
> may limit opportunities far beyond the point which obtains in American society
> today. It is only when a system of cultural values extols . . . certain *common*
> success-goals *for the population at large* while the social structure rigorously
> restricts or completely closes access to approved modes of reaching these goals
> *for a considerable part of the same population,* that deviant behavior ensues on a
> large scale . . . a cardinal American virtue, "ambition" promotes a cardinal Amer-
> ican vice, "deviant behavior."[33]

Merton postulates five forms of individual adaptation to the interaction of cultural goals and institutionalized norms: conformity, innovation, ritualism, retreatism, and rebellion. Conformity refers to
full acceptance of both goals and means; innovation, to full acceptance of the goals but with the introduction of new normative means.

While Merton's own references to blacks placed them in the category of *ritualism* ("the abandoning or scaling down of lofty cultural
goals of great pecuniary success and rapid social mobility to the
point where one's aspirations can be satisfied . . . ,")[34] many more at
this time would probably be classified as possessing the adaptive
styles of either *innovation, retreatism* ("People who are in the society but not of it . . . the true aliens . . . they have relinquished culturally prescribed goals and their behavior does not accord with institutionalized norms . . . an expedient which arises from continued
failure to near this goal by legitimate measures and from an inability
to use the illegitimate route because of internalized prohibi-
tions . . . conflict is resolved by abandoning both precipitating elements, the goals and the means . . . ")[35] or *rebellion* ("involves a

genuine transvaluation, where the direct or vicarious experience of frustration leads to full denunciating of previously prized values . . . one condemns the craving itself . . . ")[36]

Edwards essentially adapts this typology to his analysis of a sample of black college students, modified by the introduction of three value systems: black, white, and Negro.[37] The essence of the black value system, of course, is the creation and maintenance of black social and cultural authenticity with regard to every aspect of the black experience in this country, while the essence of the Negro value system is the approximation of the dominant white value system and the parallel repudiation of black authenticity.

Edwards concluded that the group of college students were either *conforming* (accepted only white and Negro goals and means), *militant* (accepted black goals but not extreme means, some white goals —"the American dream"—but not white or Negro means), or *radical activist* (accepted all black goals and even some extreme means, but neither white nor Negro goals and means). The majority of students in Edwards' sample (N=378) were militant; few were revolutionary (black goals at any price) or *anomie activist* (no obvious goals or means, though continuously enraged). It is conceivable that most of the latter two groups are self-selected out of the educational system by the time of college entrance, and they constitute the most alienated.

Unfortunately Edwards focused almost entirely on the political ideologies of these students, rather than on their attitudes toward the school curriculum. He does devote a chapter to his own view of curriculum, but his view is rather circumscribed since curriculum is discussed solely in terms of college textbook content and extracurricular activities (sports).

Variations in the coping strategies of the children and their parents can probably be observed in terms of the divergent resolutions to the values-normative practices distinction discussed by Merton and Edwards. We believe quality education for black Americans to be the actual convergence of values and normative practices in the delivery of curriculum and evaluation services in black schools, whatever the theoretical view of the general objectives for children's education. The perceived congruence is, by definition, motivating and self-enhancing to the learner. Conversely, there can be no convergence without consideration to the Afro-American historical and sociocultural milieu.

Suppression of the culture of a people is an active repudiation of their humanity. This experience leads to behaviors which are normal, but which appear maladaptive or deviant. The child who attends a school where sociocultural differences are disrespected, whose family has few rights or privileges within the social system of that school, who hears little of the history and traditions of his people, and learns nearly nothing of their achievements and competencies, will not respect that school nor his membership within the school community. He may even learn to disrespect himself, but he will surely experience a sense of estrangement. We will consider the evidence for alienation, the outcomes of which have been academic retardation and dysfunctional participation of Afro-American children in our present public schools. First, we will briefly investigate some current reinterpretations of human motivation since our emphasis is on these affective dimensions of schooling that influence the learning process.

Human Motivation and Need in Social Context

The origins of human motivation are to be found in the inherent thrust of the biological organism, and not in the unilateral sanctions of the environment. However, the environment can channel, redirect, or refine the structure and functions of human motivation, especially through its influence on self-perception. The child's evaluation of his social environment, and of the meaning and significance of his own behaviors in environmental context, will be based on whether or not that environment seems cognizant of and responsive to his felt and experienced needs. The form of his needs is determined by his social background, personal history, and developmental status. Human motivation can only be understood in view of the life cycle in social context. However, this view of motivation, in particular as related to achievement motivation, has not always been widely accepted.

Many child psychologists, experimental as well as developmental, do not find the construct "human need" to have much explanatory power. Leonard Berkowitz, for example, argues that need gratification may be necessary but it certainly is not sufficient for optimal child development.[38] He states that consideration for the child's development of inner controls and restraints through first imitation and subsequent identification is critical to appropriate socialization. The ability to defer gratification and undertake moderate risks, in combination with the individual's personal history of past successes, is associated with strong needs for achievement, and Berkowitz argues cogently that these capacities are the precursors of actual achievement behaviors.

Berkowitz, however, does not consider the rhythm and energy of the human life cycle. The notion of "human need" can refer to inherent and intrinsic regularity in the human life cycle that is independent of the specific character it may take in diverse social settings, and in response to varied socialization practices. The need for achievement is perhaps a fundamental human disposition that can be reflected differently in diverse social contexts, and even within the individual's own life cycle. There would be, therefore, no necessary relationship between "need for achievement" and socially sanctioned achievement behaviors.

Perhaps to meet the preceding conceptual problem some behavioral scientists such as Smith[39] have recently made a distinction between achievement motivation and competence motivation: the former is motivation for social approval; the latter, for purposes of meeting intrinsic standards of excellence. Presumably the latter is primarily based upon a prior inherent source of energy which propels the living organism through its own life cycle.

Critics who are more behavioristically oriented have argued either that "needs," "motives," and "values" are irrelevant as hypothetical constructs[40] because they do not add to an understanding of human behavior, or that specific attributes such as "feelings of personal control"[41] are critical precursors to achievement performance. Coleman reports[42] that inventory items such as "People like me don't have much of a chance to be successful in life," and "Every time I try to get ahead, something or somebody tries to stop me," distinguish black academic achievers from nonachievers. However, some children may report less personal control not because of continuing feelings of inadequacy that are independent of their social situation, but because less personal control is a real and meaningful dimension of their lives.[43] Although many black children appear less competent or less achievement-oriented than their white counterparts whenever specific personal characteristics are measured, there remains the question of whether the psychological processes of black children should ever be evaluated independently of sociocultural context, given the excessive caste and class restrictions that they and their families experience in America.

Measurement of a variable is to be contrasted with interpretation of its measure. With respect to measurement, consider the definition of competence offered by Alex Inkeles in an article entitled "Social Structure and the Socialization of Competence":

I will define competence as the ability effectively to attain and perform in three sets of statuses; those which one's society will normally assign one, those in the repertoire of one's social system one may appropriately aspire to, and those which one might reasonably invent or elaborate for oneself.[44]

Such a perspective upon competence, however, would exclude a sizable proportion of children and families who do not like the status to which they are assigned, who do not aspire always to what is appropriate for them, and whose dreams often would not appear reasonable given their current social milieus. The preceding definition of competence would lead neither to appropriate measurement of competence among black children, nor to a realistic interpretation of the findings of such measures.

More recently, deCharms has emphasized the general difficulty of operationalizing achievement motivation.[45] Fantasy measures, or simulated experimental situations simply do not capture all the implicit meanings of the construct. Such measurement difficulties need not restrict its use in research, but some laymen, and even professionals, have persistently utilized the concept so loosely as to characterize black children as "not motivated for learning," or as possessing a "low value for school achievement." Thus, Clark reports educators of Harlem youth say their children have aspiration levels which are either too high to be realistic or so low that without extensive compensatory aid their academic performance will continue to be mediocre:

One guidance counselor said: "The children have a poor self-image and unrealistic aspirations. If you ask them what they want to be, they will say 'a doctor,' or something like that." When asked "What would you say to a child who wanted to be a doctor?" she replied, "I would present the situation to him as it really is; show him how little possibility he has for that. I would tell him about the related fields, technicians, etc."[46]

Clarification of the concept of achievement motivation, deCharms argues, requires a return to personal knowledge, since the concept of motive derives from experiences of self-induced changes in the environment, of which the primary one is personal causation or the desire to be master of one's fate in whatever sphere of life. The problem of understanding another person's motivations ultimately leads to the more fundamental scientific problem of how one human being learns about another.

One general approach to learning about another human being may be to consider how he copes with the issues of the human life cycle, specifically in terms of the relationship between his own self, his social perceptions, and his social milieu. The process of development is one of becoming more human in an identifiable social sense. The function of any social institution servicing children is to contribute what they need to be the kind of creative adults they choose to be in their society. Whenever a social institution does not make such a contribution, it is at best irrelevant to its participants. The worst possible condition is one in which children, as they mature, are progressively dehumanized by experiences within a social institution, for this dehumanization would contribute most to the potential erosion of their selves. The implication for an educational institution is that its practices ought to be based on the human needs of black children and ought to prepare them for life first by viewing them as children of a people with a complex, dynamic, and rich sociocultural history.

Curriculum and Evaluation: The Dehumanization of Black Children

Coopersmith has reported that there are no demonstrable effects of schooling, independent of parental influences, on the self-esteem of middle-class, white American boys.[47] Presumably, in such instances the home and the school are complementary as to values and normative practices in the educational process. Data now available on black American children and families, however, suggest that there is considerable discontinuity between the home and the school. The desire for education for their children felt by many black parents, for example, is not always accompanied by the same desire by the school to educate black children, or the resources available to the parents or the school to promote educability. The evidence for alienation of black children in schools can be conveniently discussed in four areas: suppression by educators of existing social background differences and the parental protective function; and repudiation by educators of historical and cultural traditions of black peoples and of the achievements and competencies of black Americans in American society.

Suppression of Social Background Differences

Educators have for some time been aware of background differences, but they have chosen to ignore or compensate for them, rather than to develop programs responsive to them.

Reports suggest many low-income children and families do not receive adequate nutrition, shelter, or medical care.[48] Adults typically can only afford to purchase substandard foods, and in many areas only substandard foods can be purchased. Many grass-roots political movements know the importance of adequate nutrition in certain black communities; for example, both the Muslim movement[49] and the Black Panther party[50] have initiated programs to feed children and families. We quote extensively from Jean Wheeler Smith's article for a statement of the problem of adequate shelter in its most extreme form:

I think people can get loose from the fear of deciding about things that are important by trying to consider and deal with the problems of the people at the bottom . . . Once we begin to deal with the problems of these people, we will be building a fund of ways to work and resources to draw on. So that when we move on to others (maybe to people who can't afford a toilet), we will have materials and insights to work with. Figuring into this first set of people are the absolutely dirt-poor sharecroppers and day laborers in Mississippi, people whose ability to live through winter after winter with no money in those cold, crowded, rundown "shot-gun houses" is a mystery. They can't do anything more on those plantations than work hard for nothing and die. There is no possibility that helping them would be removing them from a situation where they could help themselves and pull themselves up by their bootstraps. You just have to see little babies lying on floors with flies all over them and kids trying to study in rooms with eight other people, a TV, and one dim light bulb to be certain that, whatever juggling it may take, the country's resources ought to be employed to get for these people decent places to live and some incomes. These workers, having been replaced by machines and chemicals, no longer have even the $3 a day that they once could make at picking and chopping cotton to pay for shoes for the children to go to school and for food and fuel . . . Now that the bossmen don't need their labor, they are being pressured to move off the farms. They may try to make it through the year in Mississippi or they may pull together enough money for bus fare to Chicago . . . How can we get them houses that the rain doesn't come in and that the kids don't mind bringing their friends home to? How can we repair the damage to the young people of having to stay out of school, year after year, to hoe the cotton and get it in? How can we find incomes for people who now are not needed even at $3 a day?[51]

Of course, deficiencies in nutrition and housing contribute to greater vulnerability to physical diseases. An example of the effects of both inadequate nutrition and housing is the medical problem of lead poisoning among many children in low-income urban areas.

A major implication for educators is that many low-income black children who attend "the little red schoolhouse" are literally sick, tired, and hungry. Inexpensive breakfasts and hot lunches could be essential in certain schools if staff expect attention and concentration. Medical staff should also be available to provide periodic checkups for all of the children as often as otherwise indicated. Such programs are not "extracurricular"; they are prerequisite to the curriculum since little formal learning will occur without them. Each school should have the opportunity to evaluate its own priorities in these areas. The importance of adequate provision of these services to school children in ghetto schools should not be underestimated. The importance, in addition, of providing opportunities for low-income people to learn how to meet their own needs in these and other areas also should not be underestimated.

Poor people often cannot learn what they need to know about important available resources. Harrington pointed out that the poor are often "invisible";[52] channels which are visible are frequently thought to be hostile and rejecting. Curricula for the black and the poor, in particular, must address some of the preceding issues; at present not many do.

Social status may influence familial teaching styles. Since most black Americans are working- or lower-class, variations in maternal teaching styles among mothers in low-income homes may be associated with variations in school readiness and stylistic preferences of the children. These styles have been alternatively examined in specific dyadic mother-child teaching situations, and in data on the linguistic and attitudinal behaviors of mothers. The research suggests that maternal teaching styles are correlated with children's acquisition of basic concepts.[53]

Hess has distinguished two types of maternal teaching styles that

influence cognitive competence in four-year-old black children.[54]
The *personal-subjective* style emphasizes the needs, preferences, and
interests of the child; mothers using this teaching style attended to
the orientation and preparation needed by their four-year-old children when encountering a new problem-solving situation, as well as
to the importance of making a task intrinsically rewarding to them.
Mothers with *status-normative* teaching styles tended to emphasize
their authority in engaging their children in a dyadic teaching-learn-
ing task, the authority of adults in general, and rules and regulations
in particular, as to what is good and desirable behavior for children;
they typically did not offer any rationale for their requests for specific child behaviors, while the personal-subjective mothers did.

Despite considerable interindividual variability among mothers
within each socioeconomic group, when observed in the dyadic
mother-child teaching situation low-status mothers tended to be
status-normative in their teaching styles with their children, while
higher-status mothers tended to be personal-subjective. In our research,[55] however, it was also found that within the lower socioeconomic group, mothers could be differentiated as to the personal-
subjective and status-normative control strategies (interview data),
and that children of the former demonstrated cognitive competence
in a preschool setting along the lines of standard achievement evaluations. Two important maternal factors which varied directly with the
children's achievements were the extent of openness of communication between the mother and her child (warmth, information im-
parted) and whether the mother herself had positive resources in the
black community. The education of the mother was not associated
with the preceding maternal factors, or with the children's achievements. Bee has found that black and white low-income mothers differ in teaching styles. The former had a lower rate of verbal ex-
changes with their preschool children in a quasi-natural waiting room
situation.[56]

There is a definite need for study of maternal-child teaching styles
in informal contexts, especially those in which all research subjects
will feel equally at ease. However, the important points made by this
research are that maternal teaching styles do vary, that this variation
may have implications for cognitive development, and that class and
ethnic differences are observable as to the ways parents transmit
information to, and control the behaviors of, their children.

Proshansky[57] reports that studies of preschool and kindergarten black children indicate that they are aware of skin color differences among themselves and between themselves and whites as early as age four, and that in the past Afro-American children have established a valued preference for white, rather than black or brown, skin color by the preschool age.[58] Verbalization or acknowledgment of this preference, however, decreased with increased age. Psychiatrists who observe this latter phenomenon in its most pathological form have suggested that the absence of specific verbalization of these attitudes is associated with complete and total identification with, and preference for, the physical attributes of white people.[59] The black girl and woman in this nation, in particular, have long been the victims of racism and sexism. Grier and Cobbs have suggested that the healthy narcissism of the developing black girl is systematically attacked at every stage in her development.[60] The history of assault on the bodies of black men and women, as men and women, is so formidable that it has not been reasonably discussed even by psychiatrists. There are a number of studies on the "black" personality, or on black women as mothers and matriarchs, but there are few published studies on the development of manhood or womanhood in black boys and girls or the heterosexual and social relations of black men and women.[61]

Black girls achieve academic superiority over black boys in the elementary school years,[62] just as white girls do over white boys. Unlike whites, however, black women have tended to persist in school through college more often than black men,[63] and those black women who have completed college have different objectives from white women who have completed college.[64] They are more likely to view education as essential preparation for a lifelong career in a working world, since the majority of black women work in unprotected and arduous environments.[65]

This research points to possible differences between blacks and whites in the areas of self-valuation, sex-role perceptions, and educational goals as they relate to self-perceptions. We have seen no educational program designed by urban educators to address all or any of these issues. Differences between blacks and whites along these and other such important dimensions are either ignored or suppressed. Interested educators ought to demand more information to plan relevant curriculum and guidance programs for black children.

Suppression of the Parental Protective Function

The importance of a protected or secure environment for the development of the child is accepted by behavioral scientists. However, in many urban areas families find it extremely difficult, if not impossible, to fulfill their protective function until the child reaches adulthood.[66] Rainwater depicts the world view of some black mothers thus:

a majority of mothers in the Negro slum community spend at least a part of their mature life as mothers heading a family. The Negro mother may be working . . . or an AFDC mother, but in either case she has the problems of maintaining a household, socializing her children, and achieving for herself some sense of membership in relations with other women and with men . . . she often receives her training in how to run such a household by observing her own mother manage without a husband . . . The children learn to fend for themselves . . . emergencies constantly arise . . . She may try to limit the type of activities that go on in the home, but even this she must give up as time goes on, as the children become older and less attentive to her direction . . .[67]

Regarding the educational system, low-income black parents often believe that they are not viewed as bona fide advocates for their children; some data, for example, indicate that parents from low-income black communities believe that "If I disagree with the principal there is very little I can do," and "I can do very little to improve the schools."[68] Perhaps parents are not typically viewed by educators as legitimate representatives of a sector of the school social system. Efforts of some educators to establish meaningful parental involvement in the schools have met with staunch resistance from the educational establishment.[69] If parents cannot function as advocates for their children, then they cannot protect them.

From a historic perspective, the black child has too often been compelled to submit the powers of his mind to the will of those representing the white power structure. The black child who is to learn to read with understanding has also to overcome a legacy in which his immediate ancestors were legally forbidden to read. Parents feared their ability to protect their child should he become "too smart." One has only to read the autobiographies of Frederick Douglass or Richard Wright to understand the complexity of the problem.

Many other studies of black adults indicate that they do not feel able to exercise power and influence over external events. Themes of latent or overt aggression in response to frustration, resentment, suspicion, and impotence or powerlessness consistently recur.[70] As the black child matures, the issue he confronts often is whether he will become mesmerized in his rage because of what he learns about the external world, or whether he will continue in a sustained and difficult struggle to exercise self-determination. Published autobiographies of black Americans report concern with this from the earliest remembered childhood years; all blacks, no matter what their political or social persuasion, share this dimension of the "black experience." Parents and children should be able to address issues in these dilemmas as to their desires for self-assertion and their fears of retaliation through and with the aid of the school as an educational institution.

Repudiation of the Historical and Cultural Traditions of Black Peoples

Black children have suffered enormously from ignorance of the traditions and history of black people in this country and the world at large. Howard has argued that the collective self has been removed from the historical process as well as from the historical record.[71] In a recent publication by the Anti-Defamation League of B'nai B'rith, Kane stated:

In 1949 the American Council on Education in the study of teaching materials concluded that: (A) The black American's position in contemporary society was ignored by the average textbook. (B) Most references to blacks were to the period before 1876, picturing them as slaves and bewildered freedmen and thus perpetuating the stereotype of a childlike, inferior group of people. (C) There was a lack of scientific data on man and the question of race. (D) Even more inadequate than the written material in these textbooks were the illustrations showing blacks in American life.[72]

Kane reports that in 1970 those same criticisms continued to be valid, and in 1969 he himself found that: while the black man's position in contemporary society is no longer ignored, complacent generalizations are often substituted for concrete facts with regard to his total struggle; black history prior to slavery and between 1876 and 1954 tends to be largely ignored; most texts do not reinforce the basic similarity and equality of mankind, though America is more likely to be portrayed as a pluralistic nation.

Despite several intensive surveys of social studies tests, the Afro-American is largely ignored except in the context of various "uprisings" which are presumed to reflect his deep desire to be as assimilated as other Americans. This very limited interpretation leads to a distorted perception of the relationship between black children, their families, and white America.

Leacock has examined the interaction of classroom teachers with second- and fifth-grade urban black children from low-income neighborhoods. In her book, *Teaching and Learning in City Schools,* she considers the personal-social development of the children throughout her discussion of curriculum, and it is useful to quote her analysis of textbook content in the black classrooms:

Thus the content of school readers can utterly devalue the experiences of Negro and working-class children by erasing them from the world; it poses the problem that in order to accept formal educational goals that involve mastering such material, they must devalue themselves. Further, this is often seen by teachers as the conscious intent of such materials. When asked about the failure of the school texts to portray anything familiar to the children in the all-Negro low-income school, the second-grade teacher responded that the children's backgrounds were "so limited that there's very little you can base a reader on." She felt the content of readers to be good because "it enriches their experience to read these things and talk about them. Maybe it will give them a few ideas on how they would like to live when they grow older . . . "[73]

From a broader perspective, a major implication for curriculum is that considerable effort must be made by educators to incorporate black history and thinking at all levels of instruction. Wilcox has recently provided a useful statement for educators:

To fail to educate for black humanism is merely to gradualize the destruction of black people and to turn black people against each other . . . to substitute the oppressors' values for their own. Education for black humanism asserts that: 1. All black children are human and educable. 2. Blacks hold in common African descendancy and victimization by white institutional racism. 3. To subscribe to racism and capitalism is to participate in one's own destruction and that of his own people, the largest oppressed class in America. 4. Education which effectively overlooks the aspirations and technical survival requirements of the black masses is irrelevant. 5. Education for blacks is essentially a retooling process: rehumanization, re-Africanization and decolonialization; i.e., authentic black men enjoy only one kind of freedom as a conceptual whole: a respect for native cultural differences, a resistance to all kinds of oppression, and recognition of one's right to defend his right to become who he wants to become as long as the expression of that right does not demand the oppression of others. 6. Black men have a right and an obligation to define themselves and the terms by which they will relate to others. 7. Education must become a process that educates for liberation and survival—nothing less.[74]

The preceding is a powerful mandate to those educators who would develop a viable "black studies" curriculum.[75]

It is important that Wilcox emphasizes education for black humanism. There is no reason to believe that oppressed people are any more tolerant of diversity than anyone else. Evidence points to the contrary, since low-income people are often more authoritarian in their orientations toward life than middle-income people,[76] and the majority of black people in this nation are poor. Afro-American children should learn the history of their country from varied perspectives. They should also learn about the ways of this world from the perspective of open, perceptive, knowledgeable teachers with whom they can identify.

Teacher-training programs must provide teachers who will permit black children to identify with them. The criteria for teacher selection should be aimed at choice of those teachers, black or white, who will not consciously or unconsciously reject the children's efforts toward identification, especially because they believe the children to be from a socially and culturally inferior people. Teacher training for positive acceptance of Afro-American children should be an integral part of the prospective educator's college curriculum, and it should be mandatory for inner-city teachers, along with a requirement to study African and Afro-American history.

Repudiation of the Achievements and Competencies of Black Americans

The visibility of black American scholarship to the American public has increased only in the past ten to twenty years. Kilson reports that twenty years ago only twenty percent of black college students attended white colleges and universities.[77] Panos reports that since 1964 enrollment of blacks in colleges has doubled, numbering approximately a half million, and that 59 percent of these students now attend predominantly white colleges.[78] According to Panos, 71 percent of the black students report as a reason for college attendance a desire to "Help my people," as compared with 17 percent of reporting white students. As many as 83 percent of the black students wish to "Fulfill a need for trained blacks." While both black and white students express a desire to use college to improve their own future lives, many more black students also wish to improve the quality of life of black people in America and to influence American societal values in this direction.

These young people probably assimilated these humanistic values in the context of the civil rights movement of the late 1950's and 1960's. There is little evidence to suggest that identification with previous achievements of selected black Americans influenced their life goals. Such an identification would be possible only through continued academic and nonacademic exposure in the elementary and high school years to the accomplishments of their people. Interviews with sixteen highly achieving southern black high school youth by Drake, for example, revealed that most had a desire to prove to whites that they could achieve and to improve the quality of life for themselves.[79] Most reported being influenced or inspired by some members of their immediate family or by a particularly supportive teacher; none reported being inspired by the accomplishments of other blacks in their early years. Similar observations have been made in some research currently being conducted with northern black early adolescents.[80]

Few black studies curricula have been introduced into the public schools in the formative years of black children's self-identities. Leacock and Clark have already been quoted as suggesting that many teachers of black children do not perceive them as potentially capable of learning; perhaps some of these views originate in their own lack of knowledge of significant black American accomplishments, as well as in their implicit rejection of social differences.

The reactions of teachers to academically superior black youth have also been peculiar. Leacock reports that she observed that teachers preferred the lower achievers and seemed to expect that these children should not perform well on achievement tests:

The assumption that ability, achievement, and popularity among both teachers and peers will more clearly reinforce one another in middle-income than in lower-income classrooms was borne out in the two fifth-grades under discussion. In the middle-income white school, the children toward whom the teacher felt most positive had an average IQ score some eleven points higher than those toward whom she felt negative. Those toward whom she felt neutral fell in between . . . This was not the case in the low-income Negro school. *Here the children about whom the teacher felt positive or neutral had an average IQ score almost ten points lower than those about whom she felt negative . . .*[81]

Comer[82] and Ladner[83] have argued for more research on the competencies and strengths of black people, with consideration for system deficiencies; such research would be enormously important to curricula in teacher and career guidance training programs. Noble[84] and Drake[85] have argued that career consultation is especially important for black adolescent girls who now must be employed if black families are to enjoy a certain minimal standard of living and since less than one-third of employed black women currently occupy white-collar positions. Such consultation could include reference to other achieving black men and women in their chosen fields. There is a clear need for educators to inspire black youth with, and to be themselves inspired by, the enormous struggle and thrust for life of black Americans over the past four hundred years.

Alienation of the Afro-American Child: Synthesis, Summary, and Suggestions

Evidence that the school curriculum could affect the development of children's self-perceptions is sparse and relatively recent. Minuchin *et al.*[86] report that nine-year-old, middle-class white children's self and sex-role perceptions varied with the curricular objectives (value orientations) of the schools they attended. The data presented, however, did not rule out the possibility that the parents themselves deliberately chose the respective "traditional" and "modern" schools because of perceived congruence with their current child-rearing values and practices. Wallach argues that signs of quality education (low teacher-pupil ratio among others) in the lone private school in the Minuchin study appear to be associated with more positive self-percepts, even within their presumed traditional-modern continuum of value orientation.[87]

Leacock's study and other research such as the HARYOU report suggest that black schools do not conform to the value orientations of the traditional school as typically envisioned since substandard performance in regard to acquisition of basic skills and a body of knowledge is acceptable and reinforced by normative practices. We have seen that there is no indication that black schools bear similarity to the modern school in its attention to the personal-social growth and development of Afro-American children. Black children do not receive a curriculum that enhances their personal-social development; they do not receive a curriculum that stimulates cognitive growth and development. From the perspective of normative practices, we believe that what they do receive is a substandard version of the traditional school.

The absence of a convergence of values and normative practices (our definition of quality education) in black schools, as well as the overt "signs" of quality education seems to us to promote alienation among young black pupils. Merton's analysis is, therefore, extremely relevant. Whenever a social structure is dysfunctional with regard to its own values and normative practices, the eventual response of its participants will be *anomie*. By early adolescence, many children may adapt through resignation (*ritualism*), physical and psychological "dropout" status (*retreatism*), or open and diffuse antagonism toward school and learning in the school (*rebellion*). Some who do attempt involvement in the school will try to bring practices more in line with expressed objectives or values; perhaps it is the role of those most immediately concerned with black children to broaden the base of students in this last category (*innovation*).

Some black children may be profoundly affected by an adverse educational experience. Perceived discrepancies between the self and the school may produce a deeper sense of estrangement—alienation from self—than mere role deviance. Perhaps the black child who is most alienated is the child who presently gives educators little trouble: the *conformist,* the child who initially perceives little or no discrepancy between his human needs and the present educational system, the child who is academically successful and socially marginal. This child achieves in school, but later has little personal investment or commitment within or to the society or, more precisely, the societies in which he lives. Pride in one's ethnicity, and in oneself as this overlaps with ethnicity, may decrease with increased stay in the schools for many black children, regardless of their academic status.

These normal adaptations to a dysfunctional social institution have constituted, in our opinion, deterrents to the development of academic achievement motivation in many black youth. There are no data to support this speculation; we are now conducting exploratory research. The study emphasizes the perceived effects of schooling on the self-images of some working-class black children (N=86) attending integrated schools. The seventh-grade students' styles of adaptation to the process of schooling are being examined in relation to their images of themselves, their families, and their community. Parents' perceptions of the process of schooling are also being explored. Data are available for over half of this sample as to earlier maternal child-rearing attitudes and practices, and children's preschool achievement behaviors; academic achievement data (grades, test reports) are also available for all the children from kindergarten through sixth grade. The study will not be conclusive, but it will demonstrate whether or not our analysis and approach to this complex problem has scientific merit.

Social change in black schools ought to begin with a reexamination and articulation of the educational objectives (values) for black American youth, as they exist within the ethos of diverse school communities, and a commitment to the promotion of convergence between these values and the normative practices within these schools. Specific suggestions for curriculum change mentioned earlier have to be considered in the context of the ethos and practices of particular schools. All sectors of the school community previously noted (administrators, teachers, parents, children, the community at large) should be involved in this reexamination and should experience the positive effects of their respective contributions. The potential contribution of those persons knowledgeable as to the black experience in this country, whether laymen or professionals, to the education of black children should not be underestimated.

Notes

1. HARYOU, "Youth in the Ghetto," unpublished report, Harlem Youth Opportunities Unlimited, Inc., New York, 1964, 161-244, 407-48.

2. Kenneth Clark, *Dark Ghetto* (New York: Harper and Row, 1965).

3. Diana Slaughter, "Research Evaluation of the Baldwin-King Schools Program: 1968-1970," unpublished report, Yale University Child Study Center, 1970.

4. S. Oliver Roberts *et al.*, "Longitudinal Performance of Negro American Children at Five and Ten Years on the Stanford Binet," in Roger Wilcox (ed.), *The Psychological Consequences of Being a Black American* (New York: John Wiley and Sons, 1971).

5. Diana Slaughter, "The Relation of Early Socialization Experiences to Academic Achievement in Middle Childhood among Low-income Black Children,"

paper presented at the Workshop on the "Discipline Controversy," Harold E. Jones Child Study Center, University of California, Berkeley, April 16, 1972.

6. Edmund W. Gordon and Doxey A. Wilkerson, *Compensatory Education for the Disadvantaged: Programs and Practices* (New York: College Entrance Examination Board, 1966).

7. James S. Coleman *et al.*, *Equality of Educational Opportunity* (Washington, D.C.: United States Government Printing Office, 1967); Arthur R. Jensen, "How Much Can We Boost IQ and Scholastic Achievement?" *Harvard Educational Review* 39 (Winter 1969), 1-123.

8. Paul Lauter, "The Short, Happy Life of the Adams-Morgan Community School Project," *Harvard Educational Review* 38 (Spring 1968), 235; Martin Mayer, *The Teachers' Strike* (New York: Harper and Row, 1969).

9. Eli Bower and William Hollister, *Behavioral Science Frontiers in Education* (New York: John Wiley and Sons, 1967); Jerome Bruner, *Toward a Theory of Instruction* (Cambridge, Massachusetts: Belknap Press, 1966).

10. Seymour Sarason *et al.*, *Psychology in Community Settings* (New York: John Wiley and Sons, 1966), 53-306.

11. Robert J. Havighurst and Bernice L. Neugarten, *Society and Education* (Boston: Allyn and Bacon, 1967).

12. Harry Miller and Roger Woock, *Social Foundations of Urban Education* (Hinsdale, Illinois: Dryden Press, Inc., 1970), 206.

13. *Ibid.*

14. Patricia Minuchin *et al.*, *The Psychological Impact of the School Experience* (New York: Basic Books, 1969).

15. Hannah Arendt, "The Crisis in Education," in *Between Past and Future: Eight Exercises in Political Thought* (New York: Viking Press, 1968), 189-96.

16. See M. Brewster Smith, "Competence and Socialization" in John Clausen (ed.), *Socialization and Society* (Boston: Little, Brown and Company, 1968), 270-320, for an excellent review of this literature.

17. Barbara Biber, "A Learning-Teaching Paradigm Integrating Intellectual and Affective Processes," in Bower and Hollister, *op. cit.*, 111-55; Hilda Taba, "Teaching Strategies for Cognitive Growth," in Bower and Hollister, *op. cit.*, 157-77.

18. Clark, *op. cit.*; William Kvaraceus *et al.*, *Negro Self-Concept: Implications for School and Citizenship* (New York: McGraw-Hill Book Co., 1965); Joint Committee on Health Problems in Education, "The Emotional Setting of the Classroom," in Charles C. Wilson and Elizabeth A. Wilson (eds.), *Healthful School Environment*, A Publication of the Joint Committee on Health Problems in Education of the NEA and AMA (Washington, D. C.: National Education Association, 1969), 29-42.

19. Allison Davis, *Social Class Influences upon Learning* (Cambridge, Massachusetts: Harvard University Press, 1948); Martin Deutsch, "Minority Group and Class Status as Related to Social and Personality Factors in Scholastic Achievement," in Martin Deutsch *et al.*, *The Disadvantaged Child* (New York: Basic Books, 1967), 89-132; United States Department of Health, Education, and Welfare, *Perspectives on Human Deprivation* (Washington: National Institute of Child Health and Human Development, 1968).

20. Lawrence Kohlberg and Rochelle Mayer, "Development as the Aim of Education," *Harvard Educational Review* 42 (November 1972), 449-96.

21. Biber, *op. cit.*

22. Kenneth Clark, *op. cit.*; Robert J. Havighurst, *The Public Schools of Chicago* (Chicago: Board of Education of the City of Chicago, 1964); A. Harry Passow, *Education in Depressed Areas* (New York: Bureau of Publications, Teacher's College, Columbia University, 1963); *Report of the National Advisory Commission on Civil Disorders* (New York: Bantam Books, 1968).

23. James S. Coleman, "The Concept of Equality of Educational Opportunity," *Harvard Educational Review* 38 (Winter 1968), 7-22; James S. Coleman *et al., Equality of Educational Opportunity.*

24. Kohlberg and Mayer, *op. cit.*

25. Christopher Jencks *et al., Inequality: A Reassessment of the Effect of Family and Schooling in America* (New York: Basic Books, 1972).

26. Charles Silberman, *Crisis in the Classroom* (New York: Random House, 1970).

27. The terms *operant* and *respondent* are borrowed from a recent article by David C. McClelland, "Testing for 'Competence' Rather Than 'Intelligence,' " *American Psychologist* 18 (January 1973), 1-14.

28. Jean Piaget, *The Origins of Intelligence in Children* (New York: International Universities Press, 1952); J. McVicker Hunt, *Intelligence and Experience* (New York: Ronald Press, 1961).

29. James Herndon, *The Way It Spozed to Be* (New York: Bantam Books, 1965); Jonathan Kozol, *Death at an Early Age* (New York: Bantam Books, 1968).

30. Richard Schacht, *Alienation* (New York: Doubleday and Co., Inc., 1970), 64.

31. The term *anomie* refers to individual styles of adaptation with respect to institutional value-norm discrepancies; alienation incorporates this viewpoint, as well as the inner psychological referents, and is thus preferable to us, for styles of behavior may be associated with internalized psychological referents for some individuals and not others. Alienation is, thus, a multidimensional construct whose behavioral referents must be specified by social scientists. The purpose here is not to specify all the behavioral referents of alienation, but to argue that it is a usable construct for analysis of the educational experience of black children in America.

32. Robert Merton, *Social Theory and Social Structure* (Glencoe, Illinois: Free Press, 1962), 132.

33. *Ibid.*, 146.

34. *Ibid.*, 149-50.

35. *Ibid.*, 154-55.

36. *Ibid.*, 156.

37. Harry Edwards, *Black Students* (New York: Free Press, 1970)

38. Leonard Berkowitz, *The Development of Motives and Values in the Child* (New York: Basic Books, 1964), 11-43.

39. M. B. Smith, *op. cit.*

40. B. F. Skinner, "Philogeny and Ontogeny of Behavior," *Science* 153 (September 9, 1966), 1205-13.

41. Julian Rotter, "Generalized Expectancies for Internalized versus External Control of Reinforcements," *Psychological Monographs: General and Applied* 80 (No. 609, 1966), 1-29.

42. Coleman *et al., Equality of Educational Opportunity.*

43. We are reminded here of a Columbia student who reported findings from observational time sampling of selected classrooms which used homogeneous reading groups; regardless of the children's *actual* reading level, those classified by teachers as being in the "low" reading group received considerably less attention and instructional efforts during the course of a classroom day. (Personal communication from Mrs. J. Alpert during her school psychology internship at Yale University, 1969-70.)

44. Alex Inkeles, "Social Structure and the Socialization of Competence," *Harvard Educational Review* 36 (Summer 1966), 265.

45. Richard deCharms, *Personal Causation* (New York: Academic Press, 1968), 257-358.

46. Kenneth Clark, *op. cit.* 133.

47. Stanley Coopersmith, *The Antecedents of Self Esteem* (San Francisco: W. H. Freeman, 1967).

48. *Report of the National Advisory Commission on Civil Disorders.*

49. E. U. Essien-Udom, *Black Nationalism* (New York: Dell Publishing Co., 1964).

50. Bobby Seale, *Seize the Time* (New York: Random House, 1968).

51. Jean W. Smith, "How to Help the Ones at the Bottom," *New Republic* 154 (February 5, 1966).

52. Michael Harrington, *The Other America* (Baltimore: Penguin Books, 1963).

53. Robert Hess, "Cognitive Environments of Urban Preschool Negro Children," unpublished report to the Children's Bureau, Social Security Administration, Department of Health, Education, and Welfare, 1968. See also Robert Hess and Virginia Shipman, "Early Experience and the Socialization of Cognitive Modes in Children," *Child Development* 36 (December 1965), 869-86.

54. *Ibid.*

55. Diana Slaughter, "Maternal Antecedents of the Academic Achievement Behaviors of Negro Head Start Children," unpublished Ph.D. dissertation, Committee on Human Development, University of Chicago, 1968; Diana Slaughter, "Maternal Antecedents of the Academic Achievement Behaviors of Afro-American Head Start Children," *Educational Horizons* 48 (Fall 1969), 24-28.

56. Helen Bee *et al.,* "Social Class Differences in Maternal Teaching Strategies and Speech Patterns," *Developmental Psychology* 1 (November 1969), 726-34.

57. Harold Proshansky and Peggy Newton, "The Nature and Meaning of Negro Self-identity," in Martin Deutsch, Irwin Katz, and Arthur Jensen, (eds.), *Social Class, Race and Psychological Development* (New York: Holt, Rinehart, and Winston, 1968.

58. Kenneth Clark and Mamie Clark, "Emotional Factors in Racial Identification and Preference in Negro Children," *Journal of Negro Education* 19 (Summer 1950), 341-50; Mary Ellen Goodman, *Race Awareness in Young Children* (New York: Collier, 1964); Judith Porter, *Black Child, White Child* (Cambridge, Massachusetts: Harvard University Press, 1971).

59. Abram Kardiner and Lionel Ovesey, *The Mark of Oppression* (New York: Meridian Books, 1951); Frantz Fanon, *Black Skins, White Masks* (New York: Grove Press, 1967); William Grier and Price Cobbs, *Black Rage* (New York: Bantam Books, 1968); Herbert Hendin, *Black Suicide* (New York: Basic Books, 1969).

60. Grier and Cobbs, *op. cit.*

61. See Joyce A. Ladner, *Tomorrow's Tomorrow: The Black Woman* (New York: Doubleday, 1971), for an important exception.

62. Diana Slaughter, "Research Evaluation of the Baldwin-King Schools Program: 1968-1970."

63. St. Clair Drake, "The Black University in the American Social Order," *Daedalus* 100 (Summer 1971), 833-97. Drake has reported that since 1960 this pattern has been reversed among black persons. Within the 25-34-year-old age group, the percentages of black men and women with four years of college or more are respectively 7.6 and 5.6. Within the 25-29-year-old age group, the percentages of black men and women with four years of high school or more are 60 and 52. Drake believes this change reflects the conviction of young blacks that "education is mandatory for black liberation as well as personal advancement." *Ibid.*, 861.

64. Jeanne Noble, *The Negro Woman's College Education* (New York: Teacher's College, Columbia University Press, 1956).

65. St. Clair Drake, *op. cit.*

66. Kenneth Clark, *op. cit.*

67. Lee Rainwater, "Crucible of Identity: The Negro Lower Class Family," in Talcott Parsons *et al.*, *The Negro American* (Cambridge, Massachusetts: Riverside Press, 1966), 181-84.

68. Diana Slaughter, "Parental Potency and the Achievements of Inner City Black Children," *American Journal of Orthopsychiatry* 40 (April 1970), 433-40.

69. Mayer, *op. cit.*; Lauter, *op. cit.*

70. Proshansky, *op. cit.*; Joseph Howard, "Considerations toward a Psychology of Blackness," paper presented at the 1969 annual meeting of the American Psychological Association, Washington, D.C.

71. Howard, *op. cit.*

72. Michael B. Kane, *Minorities in Textbooks* (Chicago: Quadrangle Books, Inc., 1970), 77.

73. Eleanor Leacock, *Teaching and Learning in City Schools* (New York: Basic Books, 1969), 80.

74. Quoted in Nathan Wright (ed.), *What Black Educators Are Saying* (New York: Hawthorn Books, 1970), 11.

75. Armstead Robinson, Craig Foster, and Donald Ogilvie (eds.), *Black Studies in the University: A Symposium* (New Haven, Connecticut: Yale University Press, 1969).

76. Urie Bronfenbrenner, "Socialization and Social Class through Time and Space," in Eleanor Maccoby, Theodore Newcomb, and Eugene Hartley (eds.), *Readings in Social Psychology*, 3rd ed. (New York: Holt, Rinehart, and Winston, 1958), 400-24; Essien-Udom, *op.cit.*

77. Martin Kilson, "Whither Black Higher Education?" *School Review* 81 (May 1973) 427-36.

78. Robert Panos, "Picking Winners or Developing Potential," *School Review* 81 (May 1973), 437-50.

79. Lillie Drake, "Perceived Sources of Achievement Motivation in Black Disadvantaged Students in the South," unpublished Master's paper, Department of Education, University of Chicago, September 1972.

80. The research on "Perceived Effects of Schooling upon the Self Images of Afro-American Children" is being supported by the Social Science Research Council.

81. Leacock, *op. cit.*, 136-37.

82. James Comer, "Research and the Black Backlash," *American Journal of Orthopsychiatry* 40 (January 1970), 8-11.

83. Ladner, *op. cit.*

84. Noble, *op. cit.*

85. St. Clair Drake, *op. cit.*

86. Minuchin *et al.*, *op. cit.*

87. Michael Wallach, "Essay Review: *The Psychological Impact of School Experience*," *Harvard Educational Review* 41 (May 1971), 230-39.

Epilogue

The Schools and Cultural Pluralism

Edgar G. Epps

The proper role of the schools in the socialization of Afro-American, Mexican-American, Native American, Asian-American, European-American, and mainland Puerto Rican children is a matter of great concern to social scientists, educators, and policy makers. Schools have simultaneously served both assimilative and discriminative functions in American society. Both the assimilative and discriminative forces are apparent in the monocultural curriculum of the schools and the systematic relationship between schooling and social mobility. The assimilative force has made it possible for the children of Poles, Germans, Swedes, Italians, and Irishmen to blend with descendants of earlier European immigrants. On the other hand, the discriminative force has made it extremely difficult for the children of recent immigrants and racial minorities to acquire the quality and quantity of education required for successful competition in the occupational system of an urbanized technological society.

Traditionally, American society has been willing to accept culturally different peoples if they were willing to become acculturated and reject their cultural distinctiveness. A special burden is placed upon members of groups with observable badges of discrimination such as color or other distinctive physical features, however, and there are barriers to prevent racial minorities from being integrated into the social system. For them acculturation is not enough; even those members of such groups who have shed all vestiges of their cultural ethnicity still encounter both overt and covert discrimination in nearly all aspects of their lives. Ethnic, class, and racial chauvinism permeate the American social institutions and exert a strong influence on the way individuals interact with these institutions.

The institutions of the society are designed to maintain established patterns of dominance and subordination among competing groups. The norms of the dominant groups are supported and encouraged, while those of subordinate groups are disparaged. One of the most important issues facing minority group political leaders as well as educators and scholars is that of the relative effectiveness of assimilationist and cohesiveness strategies for improving the relative social positions of specific minority groups in contemporary America. The goal of assimilation was almost universally accepted by scholars and by large segments of most ethnic communities until the late 1960's. However, one of the most important recent developments in American race relations is the emerging sense of group pride that is increasingly expressed by racial minority and national origin groups. Black power, Chicano power, and Native American power movements have stirred the ethnic consciousness of other groups.

Most of the contributors to this volume have raised questions about the implicit racism of a melting pot philosophy which assumes Anglo-European cultural superiority. Instead of the traditional view of equality of educational opportunity which stresses equal access to a single, universal school program, they advocate a pluralistic concept of equality which stresses respect for the diversity in cultural patterns and learning styles which is so widespread in America. These scholars raise serious questions about the ethical as well as the educational implications of policies that seem to devalue people who differ from the dominant group.

Some of the negative consequences of educational programs based on a melting pot philosophy are manifested in: the use of teaching techniques and materials which, though appropriate for middle-class, Anglo-European children, may be inappropriate for lower-class and non-Anglo-European children; the perpetuation of beliefs in the racial and cultural superiority of Anglo-Europeans and the inferiority of other groups; the relative absence of information about the contributions of non-Anglo-Europeans to the American heritage in textbooks and curricula and the possible impact of this omission on the self-evaluations of minority children; and the extreme difficulty parents of lower-class minority children encounter when they attempt to influence the schools as advocates for their children.

Schools cannot be isolated from the society that created them. "Thus when there are problems in the schools . . . one should look in the larger society for their source. And since bad schools . . . reflect the malaise of their environment, they can only be 'cured' when the collective life of the community is strengthened."[1] The definition of the function of the schools, formed during the period from 1830 to 1880, is based on an ethnocentric philosophy dedicated to the remodeling of citizens to conform to a single homogeneous model of acceptable behavior. The result is a system of public education that is class biased and racist. Pettigrew, in his article in this volume, concluded that "the attainment of a viable, democratic America, free from personal and institutional racism, requires extensive racial integration in all realms of life." Other authors contend that democratic education should have cultural pluralism as a goal. Cultural pluralism involves the mutual exchange of cultural content and respect for different views of reality and conceptions of man. Pluralism assumes that ethnic groups have the right to preserve their cultural heritages and also to contribute to American civic life.

Since the schools mirror the total society, we might ask if the schools are the proper institution for the task of eliminating racial and ethnic bias in America. While young minds are more easily molded, and children begin with fewer prejudices, can the effects of democratic schooling survive the negative impact of racism, segregation, and discrimination in other institutions? It seems that too much is being expected of the schools in this regard and too little is being asked of other institutions. For example, desegregation of housing would eliminate the busing controversy.

The primary concern of the contributors to this volume is how educational institutions can be changed so as to increase the potentialities of students. The types of changes considered include racial and social-class integration of students in monocultural schools; integration of students in pluralistic schools; decentralization of large school systems, with increased parental involvement (community control); and curricula reforms which would take into consideration the unique learning styles of culturally different children.

Successful integrationist strategy should result in minority children receiving education of the type and quality available to middle-class whites. This would prepare them for competition in mainstream occupations and lifestyles. However, if the integrated school does not accept the basic premises of the pluralist position and provide opportunities for cultural exchange and the development of respect for cultural and racial diversity, the educational benefits may be achieved at considerable psychic cost to individual students. The typical school with a melting pot orientation requires minority children to regard their own culture as inferior and to abandon it. The message at school is, if you do not reject the ethnic (Black, Mexican-American, Puerto Rican, American Indian, Japanese, Polish) culture, you cannot succeed. At home and in the community, becoming too much like middle-class whites makes one a traitor who thinks he is too good for his people. The necessity for a mutual exchange of cultures in the school setting is ignored by most proponents of integration. The achievement of cultural democracy will be attained when institutional change permits children to develop ethnic pride while acquiring a high-quality education. For some authors, this implies that children should develop bicultural identities that will enable them to operate effectively in both the ethnic community and the larger society.

Those who question the integrationist strategy question a number of points. First, there is considerable doubt about the willingness of the dominant group to provide widespread opportunities for true integration. True integration implies mutual respect and opportunities for the maintenance of racial identity as well as two-way cultural exchange. Second, there is concern about the costs to minority children, parents, teachers, and administrators when desegregation is carried out, as it usually is, with the objective of minimizing the costs to whites. Finally, some minority educators and scholars doubt that the experiences and training of whites have prepared them for the task of restructuring education so that it provides optimum developmental experiences for culturally different children. Minority scholars must provide the theoretical perspectives and research paradigms required for the reconceptualization of education in accordance with a pluralistic philosophy, according to this position.

While there is little disagreement about the fact that lower-class minority group children are being miseducated today, as in the past, there is little consensus as to the most effective way to eliminate such miseducation and replace it with appropriate education. One type of miseducation is manifested in the failure of American education to effectively prepare minority group children for competition in an urbanized, technological society. If one accepts an assimilationist view of American education, the problem of appropriate education for minority ethnic groups is perceived as one of making the system work for them in the same manner it works for Anglo-Europeans. This is essentially a reformist position which looks to such strategies as integration, reorganization of school financing, curriculum revision, and compensatory education to eradicate inequities in the system. Such reforms, if successful, would eliminate race and ethnicity as discriminatory factors, but leave intact those aspects of the educational system that discriminate according to social class. Since nonwhite families are more likely than white families to be found in the lower class, such reforms are not likely to eliminate group differences in social position.

Another type of miseducation is manifested in the Anglo-European bias that permeates almost all educational theory and practice. Appropriate education in a pluralistic society would begin with the development of programs that use the cultural contexts of the populations served by the schools to determine the values, goals, and content of education. The focus in some schools may be nationalistic, even separatist; in others the emphasis may be bicultural or multicultural. The objective is to utilize the diversity that exists in this society to help children learn and to encourage a healthy respect for cultural differences. Some educators propose a type of education that would help oppressed minorities develop a political consciousness and a knowledge of the social structure that will enable them to attain greater political and economic power. Advocates of this type of approach argue that education should take place within a framework that will encourage members of minority ethnic groups to work for political self-determination and economic progress in their own communities. To those who fear that such separatist strategies will lead to the development of vested interests, increased competition among ethnic groups, and continued social isolation, they reply that the vested interests, competition, and social isolation are already in existence. The educational programs being proposed are designed to improve their relative competitive position. America cannot afford an educational system that fails to educate a large segment of the population.

To improve minority education there is a need for improved curricula, better teaching, and a more equitable allocation of resources. There is also need for a strong commitment to the goals of cultural pluralism. The community and the school should work together to achieve these common goals, and schools must be more responsive to diversity in American society. If the educational system fails to respond to the needs of oppressed groups, it will continue to promote the development of a rigidly stratified, racially segregated society.

Note

1. Sarane S. Boocock, "The School as a Social Environment for Learning: Social Organization and Micro-Social Process in Education," *Sociology of Education* 46 (Winter 1973), 17.